Donated to
Waterloo High School
by
Russ Huber

WATERLOO HIGH SCHOOL LIBRARY

W9-CPL-950

WATERLOO HIGH SCHOOL LIBRARY

WATERLOO HIGH SCHOOL LIBRARY
1464 INDUSTRY RD.
ATWATER, OHIO 44201

Carrier Warfare

Other Publications:

HOW THINGS WORK
WINGS OF WAR
CREATIVE EVERYDAY COOKING
COLLECTOR'S LIBRARY OF THE UNKNOWN
CLASSICS OF WORLD WAR II
TIME-LIFE LIBRARY OF CURIOUS AND UNUSUAL FACTS
AMERICAN COUNTRY
VOYAGE THROUGH THE UNIVERSE
THE THIRD REICH
THE TIME-LIFE GARDENER'S GUIDE
MYSTERIES OF THE UNKNOWN
TIME FRAME
FIX IT YOURSELF
FITNESS, HEALTH & NUTRITION
SUCCESSFUL PARENTING
HEALTHY HOME COOKING
UNDERSTANDING COMPUTERS
LIBRARY OF NATIONS
THE ENCHANTED WORLD
THE KODAK LIBRARY OF CREATIVE PHOTOGRAPHY
GREAT MEALS IN MINUTES
THE CIVIL WAR
PLANET EARTH
COLLECTOR'S LIBRARY OF THE CIVIL WAR
THE EPIC OF FLIGHT
THE GOOD COOK
WORLD WAR II
HOME REPAIR AND IMPROVEMENT
THE OLD WEST

For information on and a full description of
any of the Time-Life Books series listed above,
please call 1-800-621-7026 or write:
Reader Information
Time-Life Customer Service
P.O. Box C-32068
Richmond, Virginia 23261-2068

WATERLOO HIGH SCHOOL LIBRARY
1464 INDUSTRY RD.
ATWATER, OHIO 44201

**THE
NEW
FACE
OF
WAR**

Carrier Warfare

359.3
CAn

BY THE EDITORS OF
TIME-LIFE BOOKS, ALEXANDRIA, VIRGINIA

CONSULTANTS

O. DAVIS BROWN, III, now retired from the U.S. Navy, has worked as a private consultant to the Navy on various projects, providing technical support for Pacific fleet exercises and the evaluation of Navy tactics and communications. A former Navy pilot, he has served as a fleet instructor, test pilot, and ship and air wing maintenance manager.

ROD FREDERIKSEN flew Sea Harriers from HMS *Hermes* during the 1982 Falklands War. Before moving to jump jets, he had accumulated over 3,000 hours' flying time, mostly in F-4 Phantoms. He is now British Aerospace's project pilot for the latest version of the Sea Harrier, the FRS2.

SENIOR CHIEF PHOTOGRAPHER'S MATE BOB LAWSON, former editor in chief of *The Hook* magazine, served one tour in Vietnam during his twenty-six years in the U.S. Navy. Now retired, he currently does freelance photojournalism and consulting work.

VICE ADMIRAL PAUL FENTON McCARTHY, recently retired from the U.S. Navy, commanded the attack carrier USS *Constellation* before becoming commander of Carrier Group One, and later of the U.S. Seventh Fleet. He has flown more than 250 combat missions during more than thirty-five years of service and currently is president of an international consulting firm.

COMMANDER DONALD W. McSWAIN, USN, works on development and acquisition of future carrier strike aircraft at the Pentagon, having flown a variety of carrier-borne aircraft for fifteen years. He served as a naval strike liaison officer on the planning staff of the Joint Force Air Component Commander during Operation Desert Shield and Operation Desert Storm.

DAVID MORGAN flew Sea Harriers for the Royal Navy during the Falkland Islands War. By the time of the conflict, he had accumulated almost 1,000 hours in the Harrier, mostly the GR3, and had just started conversion to the Sea Harrier. He is now flying Sea Harriers as a test pilot and instructor in the Royal Navy.

LIEUTENANT COMMANDER KENNETH NEUBAUER is a Navy fighter pilot with over 2,800 flight hours in the F-14, F-21, and F-4, and more than 550 carrier-arrested landings. He was the operations officer with VF-33 aboard the USS *America* during Operation Desert Storm.

LIEUTENANT COMMANDER DAVID PARSONS is a naval flight officer with over 2,000 hours in the Tomcat (F-14) and more than 650 carrier-arrested landings. He was a reconnaissance coordinator for the Red Sea Battle Force and a member of Fighter Squadron 32 aboard the USS *John F. Kennedy* during Operation Desert Storm.

COLONEL T.C. SKANCHY, recently retired from the U.S. Air Force, commanded a fighter wing and the F-15 Division, Fighter Weapons School at Nellis Air Force Base, Nevada. He also served there as the vice commander of Red Flag, the Air Force's combined air operations training program.

CONTENTS

Top Guns
at Work

On the oceans that cover two-thirds of the planet and provide the broadest of all roads to war, the aircraft carrier is a leviathan, fearsome beyond compare. A modern carrier stretches more than a thousand feet from bow to stern and holds within its vastness as many as eighty-five aircraft, virtually all of them capable of a ferocious sting. Nor does the floating airfield travel alone. Arrayed around it is a guard of about ten other ships, forming an integrated battle group spread over some 30,000 square miles of sea. Aloft, planes with powerful radar keep watch on three million cubic miles of the surrounding sky.

For all its size and scope, the world of the aircraft carrier can seem very small, an arena of split-second action and tightly rationed space. Too short to let most of its aircraft take off under their own power, the ship virtually flings them into the air with steam-driven catapults that accelerate the planes from zero to 150 knots in just two seconds. Landing blends delicacy with violence. As the carrier sails upwind through the heaving sea, the pilot must bring his plane down a precisely defined glide slope, then—in a kind of controlled crash that generates an impact force of up to eighty tons—catch an arresting wire that will wrench the aircraft to a halt in the space of about 350 feet. To do this at night and perhaps in a storm is a challenge that causes the pulses of even the most experienced pilots to race. But such moments are part of the job: More than any other military fliers, Navy pilots routinely work close to the edge of human capability.

During a catapult launch from a French carrier, a pilot endures acceleration of six times earth's gravity.

Separated by a distance of only thirty feet or so, a pair of U.S. Navy A-7E Corsairs make a diving turn.

As the pilot of an F-14 Tomcat races down a desert canyon, key information is projected on his plane's windshield in simple symbols.

Two F-14As bank toward the aircraft carrier USS *John F. Kennedy,* awaiting their turn to land. They will touch down forty-five seconds apart.

Descending toward the USS *Constellation,* a
pilot is guided down by the orange and
blue lights on the runway's left side.

Down to the Sea in Airplanes

Ammunition belt in hand, a door gunner aboard a Navy Sea King helicopter keeps a sharp lookout for terrorists, as the carrier *Dwight D. Eisenhower* transits the Suez Canal shortly after Iraq invaded Kuwait in August 1990. Launched from the carrier, the chopper was just one part of a security force that also included machine gunners aboard the carrier and teams on deck armed with infrared-homing Stinger antiaircraft missiles.

"Where are the carriers?" It was a question that counselors to the president of the United States in times of crisis had learned to anticipate. At the outbreak of hostilities in a remote yet strategically vital area, the disposition of the flattops was often the first thing the commander in chief wanted to know. So when Iraqi troops invaded the tiny oil-rich kingdom of Kuwait on August 1, 1990, the Pentagon was quick to inform the White House that there were two aircraft carriers within hailing distance of the trouble spot—the *Independence* in the Indian Ocean and the *Dwight D. Eisenhower* in the Mediterranean.

Early the following morning, at an emergency session of the National Security Council, General Norman Schwarzkopf, head of the U.S. Central Command, whose responsibilities encompassed Kuwait, emphasized to President George Bush and his advisers that the two carriers were the only U.S. military assets that could be moved within range of the Iraqis at short notice. By themselves, the fifty-five fighters and attack planes on each ship could not inflict enough punishment to force the invaders back to Baghdad, but their presence might deter Iraqi dictator Saddam Hussein from any additional depredations he might have in mind—such as sending his divisions into Saudi Arabia. On August 7, after further deliberations, Bush proclaimed Operation Desert Shield, designed to protect the vulnerable, oil-rich nation from suffering the same fate as its neighbor.

Within a few months, there would be 230,000 U.S. troops and more than a thousand warplanes based in Saudi Arabia—more than enough to dissuade Saddam from attempting another land grab. But in the opening fortnight of the buildup, the ground units and Air Force squadrons filtering into Saudi Arabia were vulnerable, and they depended on carrier power to help keep the Iraqis at bay.

Fortunately for the first U.S. troops to arrive, the flattops were primed for action from day one of Desert Shield. On the day Bush ordered the buildup, the *Independence* and its seven-ship battle group reached the Gulf of Oman—just outside the mine-strewn

Persian Gulf and close enough to Kuwait to launch air raids on enemy concentrations along the Saudi border. That evening, hours after Secretary of Defense Richard Cheney met with Egyptian President Hosni Mubarak and secured his cooperation, the *Eisenhower* entered the Suez Canal with its battle group and slipped into the Red Sea. From there, warplanes could range into western Iraq. Saddam had his guns pointed toward Saudi Arabia and may have been tempted to open fire, but the Navy threatened from two sides.

The arrival of the two flattops marked the beginning of a complicated sequence of moves that would, by the middle of January, triple the number of aircraft carriers arrayed against Iraq. By mid-August, the *Saratoga* had hastily departed Mayport, Florida, and was steaming across the Atlantic with its suite of warships to spell the *Eisenhower*, which had already been at sea for five months of a typical six-month cruise when it transited the Suez. The *Independence*, which had been at sea only three months, would be relieved in November by the *Midway*, a much-refitted 1945-vintage carrier that the Navy sent with its battle group all the way from Japan.

Meanwhile, at Norfolk, Virginia, crew members of the carrier *John F. Kennedy*, in port for a refitting scheduled to last at least until February, learned to their surprise that they too would soon be joining the Desert Shield deployment. Working on only four days' notice, Navy and civilian mechanics toiled around the clock to change every aircraft engine that had fewer than 100 hours' operating time left before the next required overhaul; some of these contract workers even offered to ship out with the *Kennedy* if needed. In the same hectic span, 700 pallets of provisions—including 835,000 pounds of meat and two million eggs—were hoisted aboard and packed into cold storage to provide for the ship's complement of nearly 3,000 sailors and its air wing of more than 2,000 men.

Some tasks simply had to be put off. There was no time to renew the antiskid coating on the *Kennedy*'s well-worn flight deck, and it would remain treacherously slick throughout the deployment. Flight crews—who were authorized to carry handguns in case they were shot down—found little time to shop for side arms more potent than the .38-caliber "peashooters" the Navy issued them. One officer with a *Kennedy* fighter squadron managed to arrange a swap with a similar outfit attached to the carrier *America*, scheduled to stand down in Norfolk until May 1991. In exchange for the six-shot revolvers, the fliers with the *America* kindly parted with their more modern Navy-issue Smith & Wesson Model 39s, 9-mm semiauto-matic pistols with eight-round magazines.

Within months, the members of that squadron would have cause to regret their generosity, for their ship also would be summoned prematurely to swell the armada off Saudi Arabia, arriving in the Red Sea by mid-January. As the *America* joined the *Saratoga* and the *Kennedy*, carrier battle groups led by the *Ranger*, dispatched from San Diego, and by the *Theodore Roosevelt*, ordered from Norfolk, took up station with the *Midway* in the Persian Gulf.

A Pentagon contingency plan for defending the Arabian peninsula—which comprises, in addition to Saudi Arabia, a half-dozen or so smaller countries—called for only three carrier battle groups. Planners deemed the additional trio necessary to implement President Bush's growing agenda: to oust the Iraqis from Kuwait by force if they refused to withdraw peaceably. This decision, ratified by the United Nations at the end of November, also brought to the region more than 400,000 American ground troops and some 1,200 U.S. Air Force fighters, bombers, and aerial tankers—plus smaller but equally resolute contingents from twenty-nine other nations.

No attempt was made to keep this massive buildup secret. Indeed, Pentagon officials hoped that Saddam would carefully weigh the punishment that allied forces, including the six aircraft-carrier battle groups, were capable of meting out if he refused to back down. Isolated in Baghdad as the UN-declared deadline for an Iraqi withdrawal approached, the dictator may never have grasped how much the presence of this armada lengthened the odds against him. The carriers doubled the number of potential axes for attacking occupied Kuwait and Iraq by air. Saddam would have to defend against raids launched not only from Saudi Arabia to the south and Turkey to the northwest but from the Red Sea and the Persian Gulf as well.

Together with the destroyers, cruisers, and supply ships that defended and supported the six carriers, the fleet totaled forty-nine ships, menacing Saddam with one of the most awesome displays of naval air and sea power ever seen. To a lesser megalomaniac, this exhibition alone might have been intimidating enough to force retreat. But Saddam would not be persuaded to go in peace—not by the carriers, not by the tanks and artillery, not by the land-based fighters and bombers all primed for action against him.

America's stunning assembly of carrier power around the Middle East crowned eight decades of technological and tactical innova-

Canopies shielded from blowing sand by makeshift leather or paper covers, F/A-18 Hornet fighter-bombers nest menacingly on the prow of the carrier *America* as it passes an Egyptian antiaircraft battery guarding the Suez Canal on January 15, 1991. Four days later, the dual-purpose Hornets would swarm off the carrier's deck to sting the Iraqis in the first of more than 1,400 sorties flown from the Red Sea by *America* squadrons during the desert war.

21

tion. In November 1910, seven years after the Wright brothers made their first flight, a civilian exhibition pilot named Eugene Ely flew a spindly biplane, pieced together from a couple of wrecks, off a wooden platform installed over the bow of the cruiser USS *Birmingham*. Ely intended to make the attempt in the middle of Norfolk harbor, with the cruiser steaming into the wind to give his craft extra lift. But when the *Birmingham* failed to raise anchor on schedule, the impatient pilot trundled off the planks of the stationary ship, skimmed the waves with his wheels, and got enough power from the engine to climb and skirt the shoreline for a few minutes before touching down safely on the beach. The following January, Ely reversed his earlier feat to accomplish another first. Taking off from San Francisco, he dropped onto temporary decking on the cruiser *Pennsylvania*, where restraining ropes tied to sandbags snared his plane and slowed it to a halt. Buoyed by the successful experiment, the captain of the *Pennsylvania* called it "the most important landing of a bird since the dove flew back to the ark."

American warship skippers welcomed the idea of shipborne aircraft for their value in reconnaissance and adjusting the aim of naval gunfire; planes could scour much vaster tracts of ocean than could lumbering cruisers and battleships, whose lookouts could see barely more than twenty miles on a clear day. In Britain, however, a few visionaries had a grander concept in mind. They foresaw ships whose primary mission would be to launch and recover aircraft sent off not only to find the enemy but to attack him as well.

In the waning months of World War I, the Royal Navy converted the cruiser *Furious* to carry aircraft by replacing the ship's forward turret with a flight deck. On July 19, 1918, seven Sopwith Camels flew eighty miles from the *Furious* to bomb a zeppelin base in northern Germany. The raid, which left the facility in ruins, demonstrated to other nations that ships carrying aircraft had great offensive potential against distant enemies that could otherwise not be attacked by air without first seizing land bases nearby.

During the two decades of uneasy peace that followed Germany's defeat, the leading naval powers—including Britain, the United States, and Japan—all built new flattops from the keel up to accommodate scores of warplanes that could swoop down on targets located far beyond the reach of the mightiest battleships.

Japan's big push yielded a stunning dividend in late 1941, when the Imperial Navy dispatched a strike force of six carriers whose

Charting the way for naval aviation, a biplane piloted by Eugene Ely approaches a temporary flight deck on the cruiser *Pennsylvania* in San Francisco Bay on January 18, 1911. Hooks attached to the plane engaged a series of ropes tied to sandbags on either side of the platform, dragging the aircraft to a halt. To protect himself during the historic landing, Ely wore a leather football helmet and inflated bicycle tubes.

dive bombers tore up the U.S. Pacific Fleet at Pearl Harbor, 4,500 miles from Tokyo. America's carriers were safely at sea with their task forces, however, and six months later three of them exacted retribution off Midway Island, where their airplanes surprised and sank four Japanese carriers at a cost of just one U.S. flattop. The victory not only tipped the balance of power in the Pacific but also demonstrated that a navy such as Japan's, which had invested its hopes in carrier power, could suffer a sudden and ruinous loss if it failed to stifle the competition. Mindful of that lesson, the U.S. Navy made sure its carrier fleet would be second to none. By 1943, American shipyards were turning out flattops at the astonishing rate of nearly one a month, amassing by war's end more than twice the number possessed by the rest of the world's navies combined.

Many of the older, smaller vessels were mothballed after V-J Day, and military planners began to wonder if long-range strategic bombers (the prototype of the intercontinental B-36 was unveiled coincidentally with victory over Japan) would render the carrier obsolete. Such thinking was flawed; long-range bombers would never have the flexibility, quick reflexes, and short flight times needed to support troops beyond the reach of land-based tactical aircraft. As if to make a case for aircraft carriers, North Korean troops invaded South Korea in June 1950 and seized the capital of Seoul. Little stood in the way of their overrunning the entire country.

President Harry Truman promptly committed the nation to the defense of South Korea—and called on the carriers to lead the effort. In September, Marines backed by warplanes from five U.S. flattops landed at Inchon and drove deep into North Korea. China saved the aggressors from a punishing defeat by committing the first of thirty divisions to the conflict in late November. As the war dragged on, carrier-borne Navy and Marine Corps squadrons kept up the pres-

The angled flight deck dramatically demonstrated its safety benefits on October 21, 1961, when an F-8 Crusader came down hard on the deck of the *Franklin D. Roosevelt* in rough seas, crushing the jet's landing gear and sparking a fire *(near right)*. Had the landing area been located behind the takeoff area, as on earlier, straight-deck carriers, the jet would have smashed into a barrier, possibly killing the pilot and endangering parked aircraft. Instead, it shot overboard *(middle)*, enabling the pilot to eject *(far right)* and escape with his life.

WATERLOO HIGH SCHOOL LIBRARY
1464 INDUSTRY RD.
ATWATER, OHIO 44201

sure relentlessly until a settlement was hammered out in 1953 that affirmed the independence of South Korea.

At the close of the Korean War, twenty-nine U.S. carriers of various dimensions were in service, but in the aftermath, the Navy moved toward a modern fleet of fifteen big flattops. Of the older ships, only the 67,500-ton *Midway*—a blockbuster by 1945 standards—would survive the transition, and she would look trim beside the newcomers. Displacing 100,000 tons and more, these supercarriers incorporated two British innovations—steam-driven catapults to thrust heavy jet aircraft aloft, and angled flight decks. Older ships without this latter feature had to park aircraft on the bow while planes landed over the stern. With planes in his way, a pilot who missed the arresting cables could not accelerate and try another landing. He could only run into a wire barrier erected to save the parked planes, almost certainly wrecking his mount and perhaps dying. By letting planes land obliquely, the angled flight deck solved this problem. In 1961, the Navy added a revolutionary nuclear power plant in the *Enterprise*, which packed enough fuel in its core to circle the globe twenty-four times without pausing.

The flexibility and endurance of the U.S. carrier force became clear during the long American involvement in Vietnam. In August 1964, after the destroyer *Maddox* was attacked by North Vietnamese torpedo boats while gathering intelligence in the Gulf of Tonkin, pilots from the *Ticonderoga* and the *Constellation* carried out the first U.S. air strikes against North Vietnam. At one time or another over the next eight and a half years, nearly every U.S. carrier saw service for up to eleven months at a stretch at either Yankee Station off North Vietnam or Dixie Station off South Vietnam.

Yankee Station was particularly important because the Navy warplanes launched from there had a shorter route to Hanoi and

other objectives in North Vietnam than did the Air Force jets dispatched from Thailand and South Vietnam. Profiting by the access only carriers could provide, Navy pilots flew some 275,000 sorties against the North during the war, compared to 226,000 by Air Force pilots. In May 1972 alone, the six carriers deployed in the Gulf of Tonkin unleashed nearly 4,000 strikes against the North as part of an aerial marathon known as Operation Linebacker, the U.S. response to North Vietnam's Easter invasion of the South.

After Vietnam, dramatic events on disparate fronts would inspire both a fresh appreciation for the offensive potential of carriers and concern for their defense. The good news for advocates of carrier power would come from an unlikely source—a British Navy that politics had forced to give up its big flattops in the 1960s. Left with only a few small carriers capable of accommodating only eight or nine vertical takeoff jump jets each, the British would nonetheless extract full value from those vessels in a daring effort to oust Argentine troops from the remote Falkland Islands in 1982.

While the Falklands campaign would confirm the ability of carriers to dominate distant theaters, it would also alert the world to an insidious new threat—guided missiles that could be fired from beyond the horizon. That menace would be of increasing concern to the U.S. Navy as its carriers sought to protect American interests in the troubled Middle East during the 1980s. Yet the Navy responded to this threat, as to other challenges, by strengthening its already formidable defenses. By the time U.S. carriers gathered in the Red Sea and the Persian Gulf as guarantors of Kuwait's independence, they would come equipped with a superior array of countermeasures that minimized the risk to vessels at the periphery of the battle group and rendered the carrier at the center of the web as secure as any capital ship could be in time of war.   ★

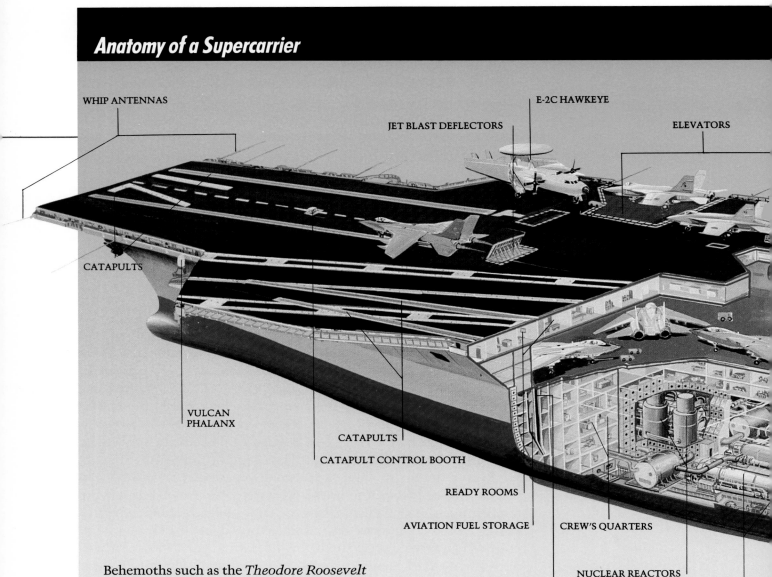

WHIP ANTENNAS

E-2C HAWKEYE

JET BLAST DEFLECTORS

ELEVATORS

CATAPULTS

VULCAN
PHALANX

CATAPULTS

CATAPULT CONTROL BOOTH

READY ROOMS

AVIATION FUEL STORAGE

CREW'S QUARTERS

NUCLEAR REACTORS

WATER STORAGE

TURBINES

Behemoths such as the *Theodore Roosevelt* extend a fifth of a mile from stem to stern and displace nearly 100,000 tons—twice the weight of the fabled German battleship *Bismarck*. Propelling the flattop at speeds in excess of thirty-five knots are four steam-driven turbines powered by twin nuclear reactors buried deep in the hull and enclosed within thick shielding to contain radiation.

Elsewhere on the lower levels of this Nimitz-class carrier lie accommodations for the crew of 6,000 and facilities to serve them, including mess halls, clinics, and radio and television stations—as well as workshops and storage areas that make this giant war machine self-sufficient.

The main business of the carrier takes place on the flight deck and on a cavernous hangar deck, where most maintenance is done; it can hold up to half the ship's aircraft. Four elevators carry planes to and from the flight deck. Here planes are launched by four steam catapults—two in the bow and two in the angled portion of the deck—and recovered by arresting gear that snares jets as they land.

Looming above the flight deck is the island, the ship's nerve center. There officers control flight operations and keep in touch with support vessels. Defenses—Sea Sparrow missiles and Phalanx guns *(pages 56-57)*—are controlled from the combat direction center, one level below the flight deck.

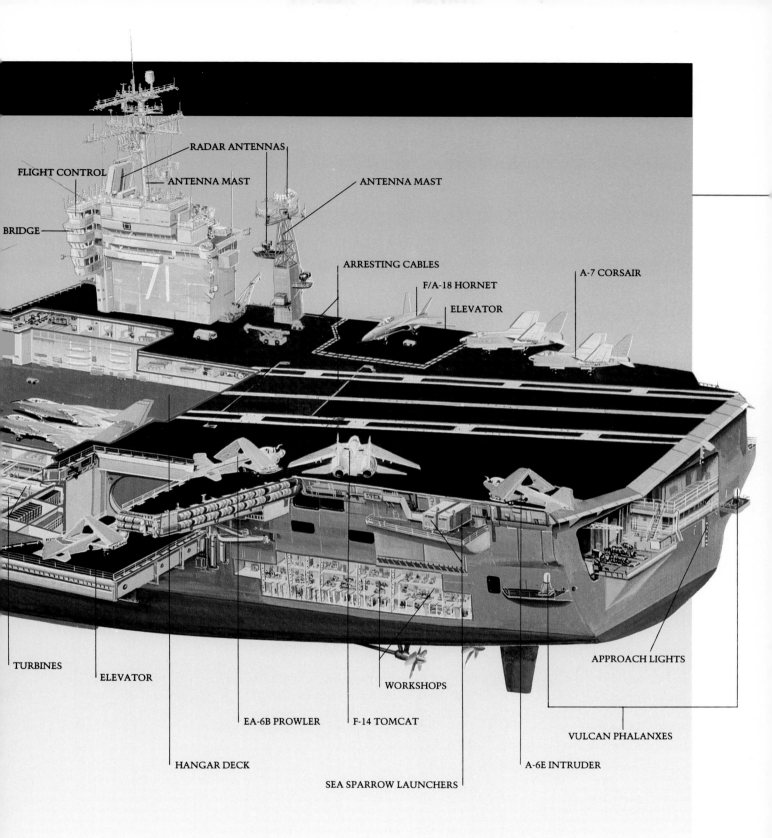

FLIGHT CONTROL

RADAR ANTENNAS

ANTENNA MAST

ANTENNA MAST

BRIDGE

ARRESTING CABLES

F/A-18 HORNET

A-7 CORSAIR

ELEVATOR

TURBINES

ELEVATOR

WORKSHOPS

APPROACH LIGHTS

EA-6B PROWLER

F-14 TOMCAT

VULCAN PHALANXES

HANGAR DECK

A-6E INTRUDER

SEA SPARROW LAUNCHERS

The Quest for a Puncture-Proof Shield

Smoke rises from the listing USS *Stark* on May 18, 1987, the day after the frigate was hit by two Exocet antiship missiles while patrolling the Persian Gulf. The Exocets touched off a fire inside the frigate so fierce that damage-control teams had to work nearly around the clock to extinguish it.

Near the horizon, far off the port bow in the nighttime distance, a pinpoint of white light caught the eye of the forward lookout on the USS *Stark*. It resembled the flash of a navigation beacon, and the lookout reported his sighting to the bridge. On this night, May 17, 1987, the 3,600-ton guided-missile frigate was in the Persian Gulf, one of seven American warships sent to deter the warring nations of Iran and Iraq from extending their wrath to neutral shipping. At the time, the *Stark* sliced through the gulf roughly at its center, eighty-five miles north of Bahrain.

Mines had been laid in the shipping lanes by the two belligerents, and the lookout turned his attention to the water immediately ahead of the frigate, trying to see any mine that might bob in front of the *Stark* in time for the ship to avoid it. When the seaman again looked to port moments later, he once more saw a light, but now it seemed a blue dot dancing on the horizon. As the seconds passed, the dot steadied. It was coming closer—fast. Horrified, he suddenly understood. "Inbound missile, inbound missile!" he screamed into the intercom. Then he hit the deck.

Ten seconds later, a sea-skimming AM-39 Exocet antiship missile, built in France and sold to Iraq, slammed into the bow. A sharp thud reverberated through the hull, leading some crewmen to think that the frigate's 76-mm gun had been fired; others wondered if a pump or some other piece of machinery had gone to pieces.

Men on duty in the *Stark*'s combat information center (CIC) reacted in stunned confusion. Deciding that the light reported by the lookout had come from something on the water's surface, they had not connected it with an Iraqi Mirage fighter-bomber, approaching from the north, that they had been tracking on radar for the preceding fifteen minutes. These capable jets of French manufacture could carry a variety of ordnance, including the radar-homing Exocet with its 350-pound warhead. By the time that the frigate's crew had warned the aircraft to turn away, it was too late. The pilot had already launched a missile at the target on his radar screen from a range of twenty-two miles.

Traveling at 600 miles per hour, the first Exocet lanced through the *Stark*'s thin plating. Although it did not explode, it severed the fire main that supplied the forward portion of the vessel. With fuel for a forty-mile flight and the rocket motor still aflame, the big missile ripped through the mailroom, barber shop, radar-equipment room, and two berthing areas, instantly incinerating three men.

A second warning from the CIC to the Iraqi aircraft, perhaps unheard, did not deter the pilot from launching another Exocet minutes after the first, this one from a range of only fifteen miles. On deck, the lookout pulled himself to his feet just in time to see another blue dot boring in on his ship. The second Exocet struck eight feet forward of the hole punched by the first one. It penetrated nearly two yards and exploded, knocking the lookout to the deck and blowing a jagged ten-by-fifteen-foot hole in the *Stark*'s hull.

Additional unburned propellant fueled the inferno now raging inside the *Stark*. Temperatures reached 3,500 degrees—hot enough to melt aluminum ladders and turn water to steam. Radiating through the hull and bulkheads, the intense heat caused flammable items in nearby compartments to burst into flames spontaneously. Flames spread upward along electrical cables, forcing crewmen to abandon the CIC and other vital areas above the fire.

Worse, the explosion destroyed three key valves needed to stanch the flow from the fire main damaged by the first missile. This water, along with that used to fight the fire, poured through damaged doors into the upper spaces of the *Stark* faster than it could drain away. Water accumulated, and the frigate listed sixteen degrees to port, causing the crew to worry that she would roll over and sink.

Captain Glenn Brindel ordered holes cut in the bulkheads so the water could spill out, and the *Stark*'s crew fought on. Slowly, they began to gain on the raging fires. By nightfall the next day, after twenty hours of heroic struggle to control the damage, the *Stark* became stable enough to be towed to an anchorage in Bahrain.

In all, thirty-seven American sailors perished in the calamity, with another twenty-one injured. Most of those killed occupied the forward berthing areas when the missiles hit. Several other seamen died of asphyxiation in the toxic smoke. Still others fell into the sea through the gash in the hull. One body, that of a man believed to have fallen overboard while fighting the blaze, was never found.

Iraq's president, Saddam Hussein, offered pro forma apologies; he agreed to compensate the families of the victims and to pay for damage to the ship. But the incident had repercussions far beyond those of an unfortunate accident to be dealt with and laid to rest.

To the navies of the world—and to the U.S. naval establishment in particular—the episode added fresh fuel to the ongoing debate over the vulnerability of surface vessels to missile attack, indeed, to many modern weapons. In the short, brutal Falklands War in 1982, the British had lost a frigate and a large container ship to air-launched Argentine Exocets. Conventional bombs sank four more vessels and damaged another nine. Now the U.S. Navy had undergone an ordeal in which it had very nearly lost one of its warships.

A Zone Defense for Aircraft Carriers

America's largest flattops have a length two and a half times that of the *Stark* and weigh thirty times as much. Against a vessel with these vital statistics, one Exocet or two might seem mere pinpricks. A chill of apprehension ran through the Pentagon at the thought of what might happen should an enemy launch a large-scale attack against one of these huge, multibillion-dollar floating airfields.

The Navy, of course, had been preoccupied with defending its carriers long before the advent of antiship missiles. In 1942, at the crucial Battle of Midway, Admiral Chester Nimitz, commander of the U.S. Pacific Fleet, relied on three carriers and their air groups for his entire offensive punch; his eight cruisers and seventeen destroyers had one responsibility: to protect the flattops from Japanese attack. In the event, U.S. naval aircraft savaged the Japanese carriers, while the U.S. carrier task force defended itself so fiercely that it suffered far less damage than the enemy. Nimitz emerged the victor; the tide of battle turned in the Pacific; and in the triumphant months to come, his idea of hard-hitting, superbly protected carrier task forces became U.S. Navy doctrine.

Though modified over the years, Nimitz's concept still forms the basis of current carrier-defense thinking. At its core is the carrier battle group, or CVBG, which for peacetime patrol and power display typically includes a carrier and its air wing—about eighty to ninety aircraft—one or two guided-missile cruisers, a seven-vessel mix of frigates and destroyers, and perhaps a fast nuclear submarine, all dedicated to the survival of the flattop. In wartime, two or more CVBGs might conduct joint operations as an immense carrier battle force. Operation Desert Storm saw at its climax four CVBGs in the Persian Gulf.

On the open ocean, a modern battle group sails in a formation covering up to 30,000 square miles, with the escort ships and aircraft arrayed around the carrier in three defensive rings. Together, they work like a series of filters that progressively eliminate attacking planes and missiles, whether fired by aircraft, surface vessel, submarine, or launch sites ashore.

The outermost ring is the hunting ground of the long-range fighters, the F-14 Tomcats on combat air patrol up to 250 miles from the group's center. Their job is to hit enemy aircraft before they can come within launch range of a carrier or its escorts.

A middle zone, about 100 miles deep, is guarded by the battle group's guided-missile destroyers and cruisers. On alert about 100 miles from the carrier, they scan the skies with powerful air-search radars, ready to launch surface-to-air missiles at any enemy missiles that, in a massive attack, survive the outer air battle.

Finally, all carriers and their escorts have close-in defenses—short-range antimissile missiles and radar-directed rapid-firing cannons. These provide a last-ditch defense against so-called leakers, missiles that manage to come within twenty miles of their targets.

During the past decade, in both Cold War computer games and shooting encounters in the Third World, U.S. carrier battle groups have been called upon to defend themselves against a variety of opponents wielding a wide range of weapons. In those confrontations, all of the CVBG defenses have come into action, often with brilliant success, and sometimes with worrisome deficiencies.

To Slay the Archer

In the summer of 1981, a U.S. Navy battle force, including the carriers *Nimitz* and *Forrestal* with an escort of fourteen other vessels, steamed into the southern Mediterranean to conduct a large-scale training exercise. The maneuvers, involving the launch of

An Aegis antiair-warfare cruiser leads the battle group of the nuclear-powered aircraft carrier *Dwight D. Eisenhower* on parade. Besides the cruiser, the formation includes four frigates, three destroyers, an ammunition ship, two oilers, and, trailing in the carrier's wake, a fleet attack submarine. Two more vessels, only occasional members of the battle group, sail at the carrier's port rear quarter: A ship called an amphibious transport dock carries a Marine assault force, and a carrier-like amphibious assault ship bears helicopters to ferry the troops ashore.

surface-to-air and air-to-air missiles at drone targets, would end after only two days, but they promised to attract worldwide attention because of their location: the northern part of the Gulf of Sidra, a 300-mile-wide body of water where the Libyan coastline dips 100 miles into Africa.

Some years before, Libya's erratic, America-hating leader, Colonel Muammar al-Qadafi, had claimed the entire gulf as his own and loudly threatened to attack any intruder. The United States, regarding anything beyond the traditional three-mile limit as international waters open to all, refused to recognize the claim. To underline this position, Washington now sent the carrier battle force into the gulf—and thus set the stage for confrontation.

On the first day of exercises, August 18, almost fifty Libyan fighters—Soviet-supplied MiG-23 Floggers and MiG-25 Foxbats, along with a number of Mirages—rose from desert airfields. Each time one of the planes entered the exercise area, F-14s flying CAP intercepted it and firmly escorted it away.

Commander Henry Kleeman was flying one of the F-14s at dawn on the second day. Shortly after six in the morning, he and Lieutenant David Venlet, his radar intercept officer (RIO), lifted smartly off the *Nimitz* in a Tomcat—call sign Fast Eagle 102—belonging to the Black Aces of Squadron VF-41. Kleeman carried a full load of armament for fleet air-defense operations: a pair of heat-seeking AIM-9 Sidewinders, two radar-guided AIM-7 Sparrows, and four AIM-54 Phoenix missiles, also radar-guided. At the heart of the Tomcat lay the supersophisticated weapons-control system whose 36-inch radar antenna could track two dozen targets out to distances of 195 miles and engage six of them simultaneously.

Under the prevailing rules of engagement, Kleeman could shoot

A Multilayered Defense

As befits so potent an instrument of attack, a carrier battle group is superbly equipped for defense. Chief among the threats to the task force are submarines attempting to sneak close for a torpedo or missile strike and enemy planes that can launch antiship missiles from hundreds of miles away. To detect such dangers, the ships and aircraft of the battle group listen beneath the waves with sonar, probe the skies with radar, and receive surveillance data from satellites passing overhead. The entire electronic information stream, along with the weapons used to fend off an assault, feeds a single integrated defensive system.

Coverage is stupendous. A battle group is spread over an area equivalent to an appreciable portion of the eastern United States *(inset)*. The umbrella of defense extends outward about 200 miles from the center and reaches vertically to 70,000 feet. The protection is organized in layers. In the outermost layer are patrolling F-14 or F/A-18 fighters, E-2C Hawkeye early-warning aircraft, sub-hunting planes such as the S-3 Viking, and nuclear attack subs. Closer in are cruisers armed with missiles to thwart a missile attack launched from the air, the sea's surface, or below the waves. Closer still, destroyers, frigates, and sonar-carrying helicopters provide a last-ditch defense against any sub that eludes the outer guardians. Absent a threat, the battle group tends to surround the carrier with defenses *(right)*, but when action looms, the ships and planes shift to meet the threat head-on *(pages 36-37)*.

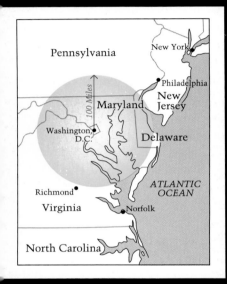

Cruising on the high seas, a carrier battle group surrounds the flattop with defenses arrayed in concentric rings, or zones. Frigates and destroyers concentrate on the submarine danger, each covering a sector of about seventy square miles as they sweep the area around the carri-

er. Cruisers equipped with the Aegis battle-management system are the primary defense against antiship missiles. Pairs of fighters fly combat air patrol (CAP) in the outer zone, positioned to intercept enemy planes before they can launch missiles at the battle group.

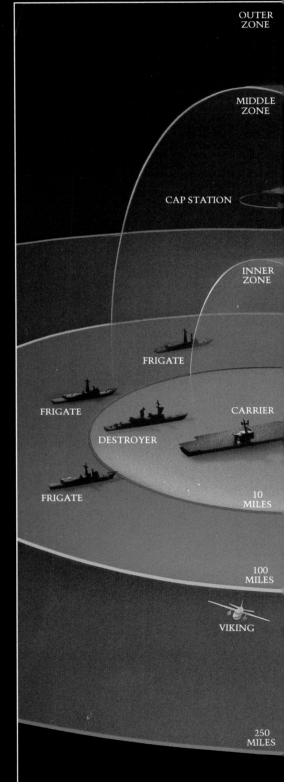

OUTER ZONE

MIDDLE ZONE

CAP STATION

INNER ZONE

FRIGATE

FRIGATE

CARRIER

DESTROYER

FRIGATE

10 MILES

100 MILES

VIKING

250 MILES

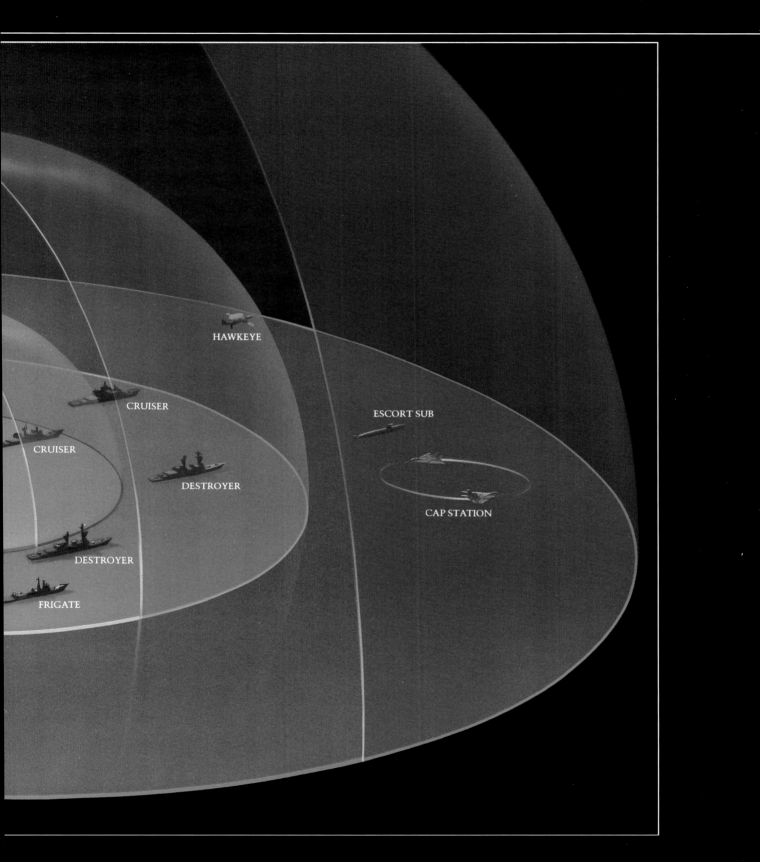

HAWKEYE

CRUISER

ESCORT SUB

CRUISER

DESTROYER

CAP STATION

DESTROYER

FRIGATE

35

Upon warning of attack, a carrier battle group concentrates its defenses along the so-called threat axis—the direction from which the raid is most likely to come. Cruisers form a picket line, ready to engage incoming missiles with their own arsenal of missiles—a task shared by destroyers. Meanwhile, the carrier shifts to the rear of the group, sends out extra E-2C Hawkeyes to help manage the expected air battle, and—when the approach of enemy aircraft is detected—dispatches additional fighters to attempt interception before antiship missiles can be launched. The greatest danger of all is a submarine attack from in close: In the scenario pictured at right, two frigates and their Seahawk helicopters deal with an enemy submarine that has penetrated the middle defense zone. The battle group's own attack sub has been assigned the responsibility of covering the rear, while a shore-based P-3 Orion looks for other hostile subs.

CAP STATION

FRIGA

ESCORT SUB

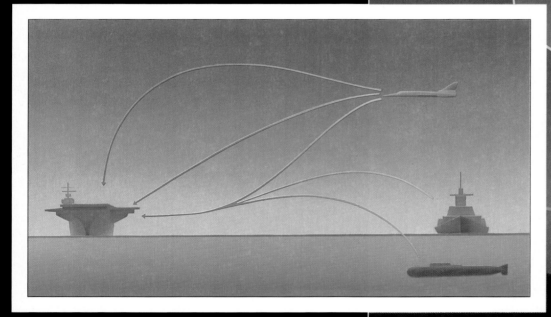

Antiship missiles that could be used against a carrier battle group form a diverse threat. They can be launched from aircraft, surface ships, and submarines. Some skim along the sea's surface; others strike from above along various trajectories. Fired from distances of as much as 200 miles, the missiles home on the target by radar and infrared sensors.

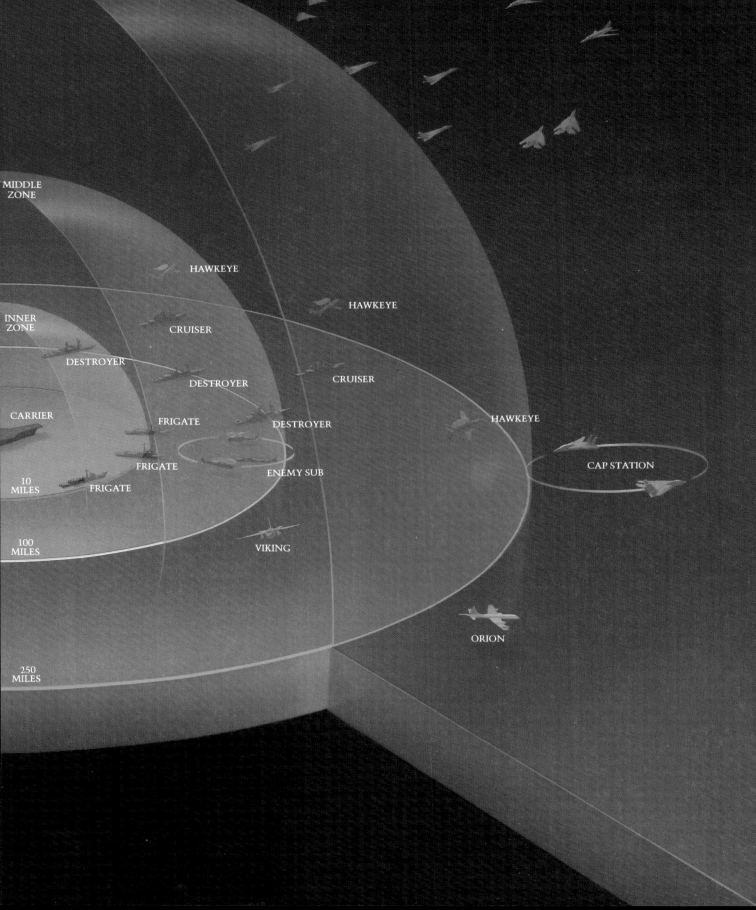

only in self-defense. If it came to that, however, his long-range Phoenix missiles could hit targets at 100 miles. His Sparrows would be effective out to 20 miles, while the nimble, "dogfighting" Sidewinder would take on the enemy from 5 miles all the way in to 3,000 feet. For close combat, the Tomcat packed a six-barrel 20-mm M-61 Gatling gun that could spew out explosive shells at the rate of 6,000 rounds per minute; the thing sounded more like a diesel locomotive's air horn than a cannon. All in all, the big (74,000-pound) but superbly maneuverable mach 2-plus Tomcats presented an imposing obstacle to potential enemies.

Wheels up, Kleeman linked up with Fast Eagle 107, Black Aces Tomcat piloted by Lieutenant Lawrence Musczynski. With Kleeman in the lead, the fighters climbed to 20,000 feet and established a CAP station about 50 miles south of the carrier, approximately midway between the battle force and the Libyan air base at Gurdabya. Ideally, Kleeman should have been 200 miles from their ship, but in the confines of the Gulf of Sidra, he could do no better.

On CAP, the Tomcats flew around in an oval pattern, with Musczynski and Kleeman always on opposite sides of the oval. As one fighter flew outbound, toward Libya, the other traveled inbound, so one plane always had its radar antenna pointing in the likely direction of trouble. For more than an hour, the Tomcats went round and round, the crews working to stay alert in the peaceful blue sky.

Then, at 7:15 a.m., Venlet, Kleeman's RIO, established radar contact with an unidentified aircraft climbing steadily toward the Tomcats from the south. Ordered to intercept by the *Nimitz*'s combat direction center, Kleeman and Musczynski went into afterburner in order to meet the bogey as far from the carrier as possible.

At a range of about eight miles, Kleeman saw not one aircraft but two—Libyan Su-22 Fitters, Soviet-built mach 2 fighter-bombers capable of carrying a wide variety of bombs and air-to-surface and air-to-air missiles. They were in close formation, no more than 500 feet apart. As the four planes closed at a combined speed of about 1,000 knots, Kleeman and Musczynski broke hard left—a routine maneuver in head-on interceptions that would place them in a commanding position behind the Fitters after they passed.

"I rolled my wings and began to turn to keep the Fitters in sight and rendezvous on them," said Kleeman, "but about 500 feet above them and 1,000 feet out in front, I observed a missile being fired." It flashed off the right wing of the lead Fitter and shot in a blur of white smoke toward Kleeman's Tomcat. The missile, approaching nearly head-on, passed harmlessly below. An early-generation Soviet-made Atoll heat seeker, it had an infrared seeker that could home on a hot engine exhaust only when fired from behind.

Now, the lead Fitter wrenched into a climbing left turn in the general direction of Musczynski, flying above and several thousand feet to the right of Kleeman. Musczynski instantly tightened the turn he had begun with his leader and dived behind the Su-22. Closing to within half a mile, Musczynski launched a single Sidewinder. It darted away from his Tomcat, flew up the Fitter's tailpipe, and detonated. Half the Libyan's tail blew off.

Meanwhile, the second Su-22 made a climbing right turn away from his leader. Kleeman rolled toward him and swung into six o'clock position on the enemy's tail, ready to finish things off with a Sidewinder. However, the Navy pilot coolly saw that he and the Fitter were aligned with the sun, whose intense heat might decoy the Sidewinder from its target. "I realized that I was not in a good position to shoot," Kleeman later recalled. "So I waited."

Trailing the Libyan as if on the end of an invisible cable, the Tomcat patiently climbed with the Fitter for about ten seconds. Then, when the Libyan finally turned, clearing the sun, Kleeman punched off his Sidewinder. It ran straight up the Su-22's tailpipe, and the plane tumbled out of control. Kleeman watched the pilot eject about five seconds later.

From start to finish, the aerial battle had lasted less than two minutes. In their first hostile action since Vietnam, U.S. pilots had won convincingly. The engagement also saw the combat debut for both the F-14 Tomcat and its tactics in defense of the carrier battle group. Both had validated themselves, though naval strategists acknowledged that the Libyans, few in number and poorly trained, had posed little threat. Nevertheless, when the Tomcats unsheathed their talons, they proved keen indeed—so sharp, in fact, that in the years since, the mere presence of F-14s has often been enough to deter potential attackers.

Seven years later, in 1988, an American naval formation found itself in a different sort of confrontation, this time with hostile surface forces. The battle group came under no active threat, and in fact mounted offensive, not defensive, operations. Even so, the action served as an example of what might occur within the middle defensive zone surrounding a carrier. This time, Iran, still bitterly at war with Iraq, became the adversary. Place of combat: the Persian Gulf, where the *Stark* had met disaster eleven months earlier. As so often for the United States, the issue involved the right of free passage through international waters.

On April 14, the guided-missile frigate *Samuel B. Roberts*, a sister ship of the *Stark*, struck an Iranian mine while on patrol in the central gulf, just east of Bahrain. Exploding under the stern, the mine lifted the ship's fantail a dozen feet, and while no one died, ten men were injured, three of them severely; only by herculean effort did the crew keep the *Roberts* afloat. The U.S. Navy prepared to retaliate without delay.

Operation Praying Mantis got under way four days later, at dawn on April 18, when four destroyers, three frigates, a cruiser, and an amphibious transport with 400 Marines moved into the southern gulf. Divided into three surface action groups, they meant to sink the Iranian frigate *Sabalan* or a comparable warship; in the bargain, they would destroy two oil-drilling platforms the Iranians had been using to attack neutral tankers and to support their minelaying operations. For air cover, four Tomcats catapulted from the carrier *Enterprise*, steaming with two escorts in the northern Arabian Sea, 120 miles away. Also aloft from the *Enterprise:* an E-2C Hawkeye airborne warning and control aircraft. Commonly called a Hummer because of the resonant drone of its twin turboprop engines, the Hawkeye slowly orbited somewhat above 20,000 feet about 50 miles southeast of the major Iranian naval and air base at Bandar Abbas, on the gulf. A twenty-four-foot-diameter radar dish slowly rotated atop the Hummer's fuselage; inside, a five-man team of specialists studied their scopes; they could see the *Enterprise* and her escorts 120 miles to the east, all of the United Arab Emirates to the south, Qatar to the southwest, and most important, about one-third of Iran, including 600 miles of coastline to the north.

No sooner had the Tomcats established a CAP station to the southwest of Bandar Abbas than the E-2C reported several Iranian F-4 Phantoms, bought from the United States in a friendlier day, taking off from the air base located there. Aboard the F-14s, pulses quickened. In the past, Iranian pilots had raced out over the southern gulf to attack oil tankers with U.S.-made Maverick missiles, television-guided weapons with a maximum range of thirteen

Seconds after launch, the solid-propellant rocket motor of an AIM-54C Phoenix missile ignites, accelerating it toward an airborne target more than 100 miles away. Guided by the F-14 Tomcat that fired it, the Phoenix quickly climbs to 100,000 feet, then coasts through the thin air at the edge of the stratosphere. During the last ten miles of the flight, the missile dives toward the target, using its own radar seeker for guidance.

miles. Now, it looked as if the American warships had been targeted, and the Tomcats made ready to protect them.

Wisely, the F-4s turned aside as they reached the coast. Ground radar operators apparently had alerted the Iranian pilots to the Tomcats, and they had no desire to fight. When a flight of F-4s veered seaward later in the day, the Hawkeye immediately picked up the change in course and vectored F-14s on CAP to intercept. As soon as the Tomcats turned nose-on, the Iranians scooted back to land.

From that point, the Americans' punitive foray against the oil platforms proceeded without interference from the air. However, the Iranian Navy soon arrived to challenge the U.S. ships with its missile boats. Events in the hours that followed would stand as a fair approximation of how a carrier battle group would deal with a surface force attempting to come within missile range.

Not finding an Iranian ship to engage, Surface Action Group Charlie—comprising the guided-missile cruiser *Wainwright* and the frigates *Bagley* and *Simpson*—had begun shelling the Sirri oil platform, about sixty-five miles northwest of Dubai, at nine o'clock. By eleven, the platform was aflame, and the ships were patrolling in the area when radar picked up the approach of an unidentified surface ship.

Aboard the *Wainwright,* Captain James Chandler, the group commander, ordered a helicopter from the *Bagley* to investigate. The chopper identified the target as the *Joshan,* a 249-ton French-made Combattante-II fast attack craft usually armed with four radar-guided Harpoon antiship missiles of American manufacture. Four launch tubes for the weapons jutted skyward just aft of the bridge. Each tube could fire one of the fifteen-foot-long missiles, which can hit surface targets at long range—as far as sixty miles away—with a 500-pound high-explosive warhead.

Ships like the *Joshan* were not covered by Chandler's orders, so he radioed the ship repeatedly, as required by the rules of engagement, that it was standing into danger and ordered the boat to depart the area. The *Joshan* kept coming. Finally, Chandler broadcast: "Stop your engines and abandon ship. I intend to sink you." At that, the *Joshan* launched a Harpoon at a range of 26,000 yards.

Immediately, the American ships, arrayed in line-abreast formation, acted to ward off the missile. From six-barrel, 130-mm chaff mortars, they hurled a number of rapid-blooming chaff cartridges 200 yards into the air. In less than four seconds, the cartridges spread countless small strips of lightweight radar-reflecting material into broad, lingering clouds, each with a radar cross section larger than that of the ship that fired it. Then the three vessels turned away from the clouds to encourage the Harpoon, now at sea-skimming altitude under the control of an inertial autopilot, to home on one of the chaff clouds when its radar seeker became active. The Harpoon passed the *Wainwright* without exploding and crashed into the sea.

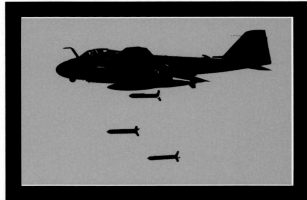

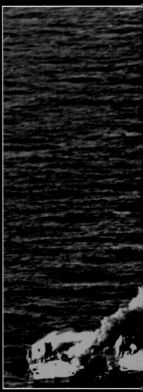

Cluster bombs from an A-6E Intruder attack plane from the carrier *Enterprise* fall on Iranian gunboats during Operation Praying Mantis, April 18, 1988. Other Intruders thwarted a gun attack on the USS *Jack Williams* and two other ships by the Iranian frigate *Sahand*. Using 1,000-pound laser-guided Skipper bombs and Harpoon antiship missiles, they left the *Sahand* dead in the water and engulfed in flames *(right)*. Hours after this picture was taken, the British-made frigate sank.

Time had run out for the *Joshan*. The *Wainwright* and the *Simpson* each brought two fourteen-foot-long SM-1 Standard missiles onto the rails of the twin launchers on their foredecks and rotated them toward the *Joshan*. Four missiles streaked aloft, hiding the launchers in roiling clouds of white smoke and drawing gnarled trails across the sky. Directed by the ships' fire-control radars, all four Standards found the mark. Each slammed into the hostile vessel and exploded, putting a sudden, fatal end to the *Joshan*'s ambitions.

Over the next seven hours, the conflict escalated as the Iranian Navy continued to sortie aggressively from its bases. At 1:00 p.m., an *Enterprise* A-6 Intruder covered by a pair of F-14 Tomcats disposed of five Iranian Boghammar-class gunboats attacking a U.S.-run oil rig off the coast of the United Arab Emirates. The A-6 sank the lead Iranian gunboat with Rockeye cluster bombs and literally drove the other four aground as they attempted to flee. Then, in midafternoon, another A-6 drew cannon and missile fire as it approached a ship that turned out to be the 1,350-ton Iranian frigate *Sahand*. Popping chaff to defeat the missiles, the A-6 hammered the frigate with a Harpoon—an air-launched version of the weapon carried by the *Joshan*—and a laser-guided bomb, leaving its target

engulfed in flames. To make certain it sank, seven more attack planes from the *Enterprise* pounded the frigate with missiles and bombs, and the destroyer *Joseph Strauss* joined in with a Harpoon of its own. Before long, the hapless *Sahand* went to the bottom.

There was more. When the Americans' first choice for retribution, the Iranian frigate *Sabalan*, appeared in the area, an A-6 sent a 500-pound laser-guided bomb neatly down her stack into the engineering spaces. Lying dead in the water, the frigate was about to be dispatched by another flight of bombers on their way from the *Enterprise* when higher authorities decided that enough was enough. They called off the strike, and the Iranians eventually towed the hulk of the *Sabalan* back to Bandar Abbas.

As a footnote, the Navy reported the presence of an observer to the show in the form of a 7,900-ton Soviet Sovremenny-class guided-missile destroyer. When, early in the operation, the warship first appeared on radar, closing at twenty-five knots, U.S. forces thought it might be an Iranian frigate. The destroyer *Merrill* prepared to launch a Harpoon attack. Meanwhile, according to the rules of engagement, a helicopter whirled out to evaluate the contact and reported back enough details, including the hull number, to identify the destroyer as Soviet. Asked to state his intentions, the skipper reportedly replied in heavily accented English: "I want to take pictures for history."

From their ringside seat, the Soviets learned that U.S. tactics and weaponry worked supremely well against modest, piecemeal attacks such as an adversary like Iran might launch. As to the effectiveness of U.S. carrier defenses against an all-out assault by a more powerful enemy, Operation Praying Mantis was mute. Soviet anticarrier doctrine, for example, has stood on the principle of victory through saturation—the same conviction long held by the Red Army and Air Force. Though the likelihood of superpower military confrontation has faded, a major conflict undoubtedly would have included an attack on U.S. carrier forces by dozens of land-based supersonic Blackjack and Backfire bombers, each carrying one or two antiship missiles. Preceded by Tu-95 reconnaissance aircraft sent to search out the carriers and their escorts, the bombers would approach from several points of the compass and release their missiles simultaneously. With the carriers thus engaged, dozens of Soviet surface ships and submarines would close quickly to launch another round of missiles timed to overwhelm the defense.

Battle group tactics against such an attack would be to destroy as many bombers and cruise missiles as possible with the F-14 Tomcats of the outer defense zone. Then the salvation of the carriers would rest with the weapons of the surface escorts defending the middle ring between 100 miles and about 10 miles from the carrier.

A battle-management system known as Aegis—after the great shield of Zeus—coordinates the activities of these ships so that they do not unnecessarily gang up on targets or overlook any. Installed on Ticonderoga-class guided-missile cruisers and Arleigh Burke-class guided-missile destroyers, the Aegis system is built around the remarkable SPY-1 radar, which can automatically track hundreds of targets at the same time, even those traveling five times the speed of sound and those as small as a basketball. Instead of the single, rotating antenna of a traditional radar, the SPY-1 employs four fixed antennas. Each covers 100 degrees of the horizon, so the cruiser can simultaneously look in all directions—an absolute necessity for tracking targets like missiles that can move great distances in the time it takes a rotating radar dish to turn 360 degrees.

Each of the four SPY-1 antennas contains 4,400 transmitters, each of which projects a pencil-thin radar beam. Through complex signal-scheduling techniques, four computers—one for each antenna—can use the beams to track surface or aerial targets that have already been detected, updating the position of each at least once a second, while simultaneously scanning for new ones.

Operators report that the radar sees virtually everything. When the *Ticonderoga,* lead ship of the class, deployed off Lebanon in 1983 to support air strikes launched from the carriers *John F. Kennedy* and *Independence* against Syrian and terrorist positions, the cruiser's Aegis system tracked not only the planes going in but also the surface-to-air missiles that shot down two of them, the debris from the warhead explosions, and even the trajectories of the ejection seats as the aircrews bailed out.

Working by itself, the SPY-1, like all shipborne radars, is almost blind against targets that are below the horizon. Aegis cruisers overcome this weakness by operating with E-2C Hawkeyes, U.S. Air Force E-3 AWACS, and other radar-equipped aircraft, such as Tomcats flying CAP. Employing the Naval Tactical Data System (NTDS), a high-speed digital communications channel called a datalink, the aircraft send radar images from their own gear back to the Aegis system, which tracks the contacts as if they had been made by the SPY-1.

Just how far the Aegis system can extend the horizon was amply demonstrated in 1991 during Desert Storm, when the *Ticonderoga* patrolled the Red Sea as part of a thirty-ship battle force that included the carriers *America, Saratoga,* and *Kennedy.* Thanks to orbiting Hawkeyes and Air Force AWACS, crewmen in the ship's CIC could track aircraft flying as far away as Greece, almost 900 miles to the northwest.

Indeed, the coverage Aegis cruisers can provide is so comprehensive that carriers can turn off their own radars and rely entirely on Aegis to detect incoming threats. By not announcing its presence with radar signals, a flattop can seem almost to disappear. During exercises in the Norwegian Sea in the mid-1980s, the *America* pulled this trick on Soviet Bear reconnaissance planes while sailing in one of Norway's larger fjords. Meanwhile, an Aegis cruiser operating hundreds of miles to the north in concert with airborne early-warning planes assiduously tracked the Soviet Bears as they left bases on the Kola Peninsula and reported their approach to the

America. When the carrier's F-14s sortied to intercept, the Soviets had no idea of where the Tomcats had come from.

Computers process information gathered not only by the SPY-1 but by other sensors that include its own and other ships' antisubmarine sonar, and relay it to the CIC, a large, windowless compartment located within the *Ticonderoga*'s forward deckhouse. There, the data is displayed on four large rectangular screens mounted on a bulkhead at one end of the compartment *(right)* and at thirty-six smaller consoles arranged in rows at the opposite end. Some display such information as the status of weapons and electronic countermeasures gear. Others are manned by specialists in the three classes of combat that might confront the battle group: antisubmarine, antisurface, and antiair.

Three air-intercept controllers, who direct the battle group's F-14s, monitor twelve of these consoles. "When I see a radar contact on my sensor, another shipborne sensor, or an aircraft sensor and I don't know who he is and he's maybe 400 or 500 miles away, coming in toward the carrier," a controller on the *Ticonderoga* said, "I may ask that a Tomcat go check him out—visually identify him. If he's a guy I'm concerned about—a Soviet Tu-95 Bear reconnaissance airplane, for example—I may have that Tomcat just sit on his wing and escort him wherever he goes. Just to say, 'If you do something stupid or threaten me, I'm sitting here on your wing and your life expectancy is severely reduced.' "

When the ship is at battle stations, the captain typically occupies a seat in the center of the CIC, facing the four large screens. Simple shapes show the position of every surface ship, submarine, and aircraft in relationship to the cruiser. Circles represent friendlies, diamonds the enemy. Squares are unidentified contacts. As long as only a few targets appear on-screen, the captain will have sufficient time to evaluate them personally and recommend a response to the battle group commander aboard the carrier. If scores of threats appear—waves of hostile bombers followed by missile-equipped surface ships and submarines—the screen will quickly become cluttered with too much data for the human brain to handle.

Should that happen, the captain inserts a key into one of the weapons-control consoles and switches the Aegis system to automatic. In this mode, the computer, not the captain, evaluates the targets according to a threat-analysis program and decides which ones pose the gravest threat and which ship is in the best position

The Eyes of Aegis

In this view of the Aegis cruiser *San Jacinto* transiting the Suez Canal in September 1990, two of the ship's four octagonal SPY-1 phased-array radar antennas are visible: one below the bridge, pointing forward; another on the superstructure aft, facing to port. Together, the twelve-foot-tall devices provide 360-degree radar coverage extending 200 miles. The Aegis combat system can coordinate attacks by aircraft and other ships with the firing of its own Standard antiaircraft missiles, Tomahawk cruise missiles, and ASROC antisubmarine rockets. These reside directly aft of the forward five-inch gun mount in a sixty-one-cell vertical launch system (VLS), outlined in yellow. A similar VLS aft holds additional weapons.

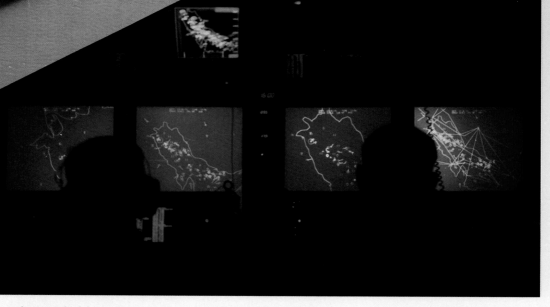

Photographed during Operation Desert Storm, radar displays in an Aegis cruiser's combat information center show contacts made by the SPY-1 system and by friendly aircraft and surface ships. From left to right, one screen displays air and surface contacts within 100 miles of Kuwait City, while stacked displays show two overviews of Persian Gulf air and surface activity. The next screen focuses on the northern half of the Persian Gulf. At far right, a fifth display superimposes commercial flight routes on the radar contacts.

to counter them. By datalink, the Aegis system assigns some bogeys to other ships, which then fire on them, ignoring all others. The computer also launches the *Ticonderoga*'s own long-range Standard missiles at targets that come its way, which may include an incoming missile as well as an approaching aircraft or warship.

The cruiser can fire a missile every three seconds, a feat made possible by the Standard's guidance system. Using an inertial navigation system programmed at launch with the target's predicted location at interception, the Standard travels on its own until a few seconds before impact. Then, using tracking data gathered by the SPY-1, one of four fire-control radars on the *Ticonderoga* briefly illuminates the bogey, and the missile homes on the reflected radar energy. Aegis interprets debris detected by the SPY-1 radar at the point where the missile disappears from the scope as evidence of a target's demise. So intent is the system on not letting an enemy missile, say, leak through to the carrier, that it has engaged some targets a second time when the computer needed a few extra microseconds to issue its kill evaluation.

If East-West strains continue to subside, the chances of a commander ever having to set the Aegis system on automatic in combat will grow increasingly remote. Instead, analysts foresee limited engagements in a variety of situations where the human factor will play a key role. The USS *Vincennes*, a sister ship of the *Ticonderoga*, had such an experience in July of 1988—and the anguishing outcome bore testimony to the limitations not so much of the system but of the men who operate it.

The *Vincennes* had been sent to the Persian Gulf region on May 16; Iran had been detected building a missile base south of Kuhestak, on the north shore of the sixty-mile-wide Strait of Hormuz, the entrance to the gulf. From this site, the Iranians could threaten any ship passing into or out of the gulf. Stationed at the western end of the strait, about fifty miles southwest of Bandar Abbas, the cruiser had orders to monitor the site and stand ready to destroy any missiles the Iranians might launch.

The USS *America* steams alongside the steep northern wall of Norway's Vestfjord during a 1985 exercise. With sea room enough for an entire carrier battle group to maneuver, fjords make ideal places from which to launch an attack; hostile radar searching for the ships from the air cannot distinguish them from the strong echo returned by the massive, stony cliffs.

Two SM-2 Standard missiles soar from the forward vertical launch system of the Aegis cruiser *Bunker Hill* as a third blasts off during sea trials in 1986. Designed to intercept supersonic antiship missiles that dive nearly straight down at their targets from extremely high altitudes, the single-stage Standard can rocket to 80,000 feet; a two-stage version can reach 100,000 feet.

Around 10:00 a.m. on July 3, the commanding officer of the *Vincennes*, Captain Will C. Rogers III, learned that three Iranian gunboats armed with machine guns and rocket launchers were attacking a neutral oil tanker. He sent one of his two SH-60B Seahawk helicopters to investigate, then maneuvered the cruiser to drive off the small craft. Instead of retreating, however, the Iranians took the Seahawk under fire, starting a wild, high-speed skirmish.

About the same time, antiair specialists in the cruiser's CIC noted two aircraft approaching. One turned out to be an Iranian P-3 Orion, a U.S.-built turboprop patrol plane. Although it posed no serious threat by itself, the P-3 could relay targeting information to a second aircraft, perhaps a Harpoon-armed fighter-bomber.

While the *Vincennes* engaged the gunboats, sinking two, the P-3 closed to a distance of forty miles. When challenged by radio, the pilot replied that he would be coming no closer. Yet even at that range, the Orion's radar could target the American cruiser. On board the *Vincennes*, the men in the CIC began to feel uneasy.

Tensions rose a notch at 10:47, when radar detected a second aircraft lifting off from Bandar Abbas and setting a course for the *Vincennes*. Knowing that the airfield was home to civil as well as military aircraft, Rogers had a crew member check the airlines' schedules to determine if the plane might be a commercial flight. The sailor found nothing that could correspond to the new contact.

Rogers next ordered the bogey interrogated by the *Vincennes*'s identification-friend-or-foe (IFF) system. Instantly, a coded radio signal called an interrogator automatically triggered a transponder, carried in the belly of commercial as well as military aircraft, to broadcast a recognition signal. Instead of a single response, there came two. One transmission identified the plane as an Iranian commercial airliner; the other matched that used by Iranian F-14s acquired years earlier from the United States. Tomcats are not attack planes, but their cannons could do great damage, and given Iran's hatred of the United States, the *Vincennes* had to consider the possibility of a kamikaze-style attack.

Still embroiled in hot surface action, the *Vincennes* broadcast warnings to the plane over both civil and military distress frequencies: "Unidentified Iranian aircraft on course 203, speed 303, altitude 4,000, this is U.S. naval warship bearing 205, forty miles from you. You are approaching U.S. naval warship operating in international waters. Request you state your intentions." No response.

Anxiety mounted inside the CIC. Sitting at a console that showed the range to the approaching aircraft, the *Vincennes's* tactical information coordinator (TIC), who had little experience in the position, became preoccupied with the notion that the captain was concentrating too heavily on the gunboats. In time, the TIC grew so fretful that he misread his own information display. He interpreted the steadily decreasing range numbers as the target's altitude and called out that the plane was descending at a rate of 1,000 feet per mile—a flight profile that suggested a warplane pointing its nose at its target as if preparing to attack.

As the bogey drew nearer, the antiaircraft warfare officer, responsible for firing the *Vincennes's* Standard missiles, recognized that the aircraft would soon be too close to engage with his weapons. (For safety, a Standard must fly at least six miles before it becomes armed.) The officer requested permission to fire as soon as the target came within twenty miles, the distance at which the rules of engagement permitted Rogers to launch on his own authority.

Captain Rogers hesitated, fully enveloped by the fog of war. He meant to avoid the fate of the *Stark,* which had suffered two Exocet hits because its skipper had waited too long. Yet he could not be certain that his ship faced imminent attack. At 10:51, as the bogey crossed the twenty-mile mark, Rogers ordered the radar contact labeled "incoming hostile." Even then, the captain hoped that the plane would turn away. Another warning went to the aircraft: "You are standing into danger and may be subject to U.S.N. defensive measures. Request you alter course." As before, no response.

At 10:54, the target had closed to within nine miles of the *Vincennes.* Time and options running out, Rogers gave the order to fire. Two Standard missiles leaped off the rails of the cruiser's forward launcher and flashed into the murky sky. Seventeen seconds later, the computer-generated symbol for the target and its tracking line vanished from the blue displays in the CIC. A cheer went up.

But minutes later, the Iranians reported the horrible truth. Instead of an Iranian warplane, the missiles had shattered an Iran Air jetliner, a European-made Airbus A300 making a regularly scheduled commercial flight from Bandar Abbas to Dubai with 290 passengers and crew on board. The pilot, a seventeen-year veteran of the airline, had made the 125-mile milk run many times before. Apparently, he had grown weary of the constant challenges from U.S. warships in the gulf and had chosen to ignore the warnings broadcast by the *Vincennes*. He might have felt differently had anyone informed him before takeoff that his course would carry him directly over a firefight between American and Iranian warships in the Strait of Hormuz.

Human factors weighed heavily on board the *Vincennes*, as well. Under pressure, a seaman had misread an airline schedule. Under pressure, the tactical information controller had misread decreasing range for diminishing altitude. Both errors contributed to Captain Rogers's decision to fire. In the aftermath, observers also questioned the inability of the Aegis radar to tell the difference between a fighter and an airliner with four times the wingspan and six times the bulk. Yet, the SPY-1 had worked perfectly within its technological limits; it was never intended to distinguish planes according to size—and certainly not by type.

Rogers told his superiors that he would carry the cross of the tragedy for the rest of his life. "But under the circumstances and considering all the information available to me at the moment," he continued, "I took this action to defend my ship and my crew."

If the target had turned out to be an Iranian fighter and if Rogers had allowed it to pass inside the minimum engagement range of his Standard missiles, the *Vincennes*, like the carriers it is designed to defend, would have been down to its last resort—the close-in defensive shield of short-range guns, missiles, and decoys.

Like the Aegis system, the carrier battle group's inner defense ring—the equivalent of hand-to-hand combat—has not been tested against an enemy. Yet an approximation of that scenario came to life on the morning of February 25, 1991, during Operation Desert Storm, as the 57,000-ton battleship *Missouri* fired its nine huge sixteen-inch guns in support of troops advancing toward Kuwait City. Since the beginning of the month, the *Missouri* had been sailing the Persian Gulf, pumping 2,500-pound shells into Iraqi positions outside the Kuwaiti capital and on tiny Faylaka Island, just to the east. Now, with the ground war under way, the bombardment took on a special urgency, and the flash and roar of the battleship's great guns shattered the predawn quiet.

On board the battlewagon and its escorts—the Royal Navy destroyer *Gloucester* and the U.S. frigate *Jarrett*—an array of radar antennas methodically rotated, searching for an Iraqi response. Sad-

TARGET-
ACQUISITION
RADAR

AIR-TRAFFIC
CONTROL
RADAR

AIR-SEARCH
RADAR

SEA
SPARROW
DIRECTORS

RADAR
WARNING
RECEIVER

SURFACE-
SEARCH
RADAR

AIR-SEARCH
RADAR

SEA
SPARROW
DIRECTORS

dam Hussein's air force and navy presented no threat, one having opted out of the war and the other largely destroyed, but a missile attack from land posed a definite danger. Intelligence had reported that the Iraqis still had as many as six missile batteries in the Kuwait area from which they could fire Chinese-made Silkworm missiles. Though primitive, each of the three-ton, twenty-three-foot-long, radar-guided Silkworms carried a 500-pound high-explosive warhead and had a maximum range of about fifty miles—more than enough to reach the fire-support group.

The attack came at 4:50 a.m. Operators manning the *Gloucester*'s radar system picked up two swift, low-flying contacts coming off the nearby Kuwaiti coast. Commander Philip Wilcocks, the destroyer's captain, sensed Silkworms and ordered the *Jarrett* and the *Missouri* alerted immediately. All three warships readied their Phalanx close-in weapon systems (CIWS). The *Missouri* boasted

Antennas atop the island of the *Abraham Lincoln* do more than control air traffic winging to and from the carrier. Also to be found in the thicket are surface-search radars for navigation, receivers to detect enemy missile radar, a target-acquisition radar to pinpoint incoming missiles for the ship's Sea Sparrows, and pairs of barrel-shaped directors to guide them.

four of the thimble-shaped units, the *Jarrett* one, and the *Gloucester* two. Each employs a rapid-response radar to detect and track incoming airborne and surface targets. To destroy them, each Phalanx has a six-barrel 20-mm Gatling gun that, firing at the rate of 3,000 rounds a minute, puts up a virtual wall of superheavy depleted uranium or tungsten slugs. Maximum effective range is 1,500 yards.

Normally, the system is kept on standby to prevent it from accidentally engaging friendly airplanes or surface craft. In that mode, the Phalanx cannot fire without permission from an operator in the CIC—the so-called man in the loop. On automatic, however, the system fires at any radar contact that comes in range. Under imminent threat from missiles, operators of all the three ships' seven systems switched them to automatic.

Within seconds, it became clear that one of the Silkworms had malfunctioned and splashed into the gulf. However, the second missile remained on course. The *Missouri* instantly sent up a volley of chaff from its battery of eight chaff mortars and started an emergency turn as the *Wainright* had done in the fight with the Iranian missile boat *Joshan*.

Yet war is nothing if not unpredictable. Diligently scanning the sky in search of intruders, the CIWS on the nearby *Jarrett* detected the cylindrical, four-foot-long chaff cartridges as soon as they left the *Missouri*'s mortars. Within a fraction of a second, the system's computer determined that some of the rounds were headed its way and in range, reflexively swung the six-barrel gun toward them, and opened fire.

At first, the Phalanx missed the chaff cartridges. Yet in less than four seconds, its electronic brain had re-aimed the gun using radar data, and it shredded several of the canisters before they could detonate to form their clouds of chaff. A few of the 20-mm rounds peppered the *Missouri*, causing minor damage but no casualties.

Meanwhile, the *Gloucester* had taken action of its own against the rapidly closing Silkworm. Moments after the original contact, Commander Wilcocks ordered two Sea Dart surface-to-air missiles prepared for launch. Automatically, a pair of the fourteen-foot-long weapons slid up the rails of a twin launcher located on the ship's foredeck. Each of the 1,210-pound missiles has a range of more than fifty miles and, like its U.S. Navy equivalent, the Sea Sparrow, uses a radar signal from the ship to find its target. The petty officer responsible for launching the Sea Darts reported that the ship's

An incoming Walleye glide bomb explodes about
900 feet from a Phalanx close-in weapon system,
scattering debris across the surface of the water.
Phalanx works automatically. As shown in the
illustration below, a search radar in its dome ro-
tates continuously, sending a beam one mile in
all directions. A computer instructs the system
to ignore any object producing echoes inconsist-
ent with the speed and course of an approaching
missile, bomb, or aircraft. In those cases, the hy-
draulically powered unit swivels to point its
tracking radar and six-barrel Gatling gun at the
intruder. When the tracking radar locks onto the
target, the gun opens fire, letting off short bursts
of projectiles that the radar tracks as well. After
each volley, the computer calculates the difference between the path of the outgoing rounds
and that of the incoming target and re-aims the
gun, continually improving its accuracy. The
Phalanx will keep shooting until it destroys the
target or empties the 1,500-round magazine.

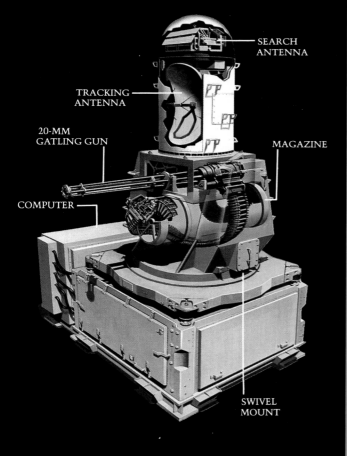

SEARCH
ANTENNA

TRACKING
ANTENNA

20-MM
GATLING GUN

MAGAZINE

COMPUTER

SWIVEL
MOUNT

radar had successfully locked onto the Silkworm. Now the launcher pointed the noses of the Sea Darts toward the missile skimming the waves, only about sixty seconds away from the ships.

With 35,000 pounds of rocket thrust apiece, the two Sea Darts blasted off their rails; four rectangular tail fins pivoted outward and locked into place on each missile; and within three seconds, the missile interceptors were streaking toward the oncoming Silkworm at twice the speed of sound.

Royal Marines stationed on the *Gloucester*'s helicopter flight deck felt the destroyer shudder slightly as the Sea Darts launched and raced westward into the darkness. "I didn't know what to do," said one Marine. "I didn't know whether I should lie down or not." Moments later, they observed a bright blue flash near the horizon. At least one of the Sea Darts, they assumed, had hit the mark. Nearby, crewmen on board the HMS *Brave,* another Royal Navy frigate, confirmed what the Marines had surmised. They watched as the wreckage of the Silkworm and the Sea Darts tumbled into the gulf barely four miles short of the *Missouri.*

On this occasion, as in the earlier actions, the weapons and tactics of triple-layered defense had worked generally as advertised. The missing factor in the equation was the submarine, perhaps the stealthiest and potentially the most dangerous of all the weapons arrayed against a carrier and its battle group.

Guarding against Attackers from the Deep

A Soviet shadow, the first of many, appeared as the USS *Kitty Hawk,* sailing from Pearl Harbor, approached the big American naval base at Subic Bay in the Philippines. The date was February 20, 1984, before the wind-down of the Cold War, and in those days, the U.S. and Soviet navies operated "eyeball to eyeball," as one American admiral has said. Three times that Monday, long-range Tu-95 Bear reconnaissance planes approached the aircraft carrier. As always, F-14 Tomcats rose to intercept the Bears and escort them about their business.

From that initial contact, the Soviets monitored the *Kitty Hawk*'s every move. In mid-March, the carrier, accompanied by her eight-ship battle group, entered the Sea of Japan to participate in Team Spirit, a joint U.S.-South Korean exercise. For these ma-

**A Sea Sparrow bursts from a
launcher located just below the
flight deck on the port side of
the *Midway,* smashing through
the cover that protects the missile until launch. The covers
shown here have been painted
with the *Midway's* coat of arms
as well as the ship's identifier,
CV-41, which pairs the Navy
code for a conventionally powered (oil-fired) carrier with the
ship's number, 41.**

neuvers, the aircraft
carrier's station lay only 500 miles south of
Vladivostok, the USSR's primary Pacific naval base.

As expected, Soviet surveillance mounted—in the air, on the sea,
and most particularly beneath it. A Soviet Kara-class guided-missile
cruiser, the 9,700-ton *Petropavlovsk,* stood waiting as gatekeeper
on March 19, when the *Kitty Hawk* sortied from Pusan, South
Korea, to take up her exercise position. For the next three days,
other ships matched her move for move. Wave after wave of aircraft,
a few pointedly carrying antiship missiles, lifted off from Soviet
airfields to stage mock attacks along various axes on the American

A wildfire on the crowded flight deck of the USS *Enterprise* cooks off a 500-pound bomb carried by an F-4 Phantom on January 14, 1969. Although a similar fire eighteen months earlier had knocked the aircraft carrier *Forrestal* out of the war, the *Enterprise*'s crew was able to contain the blaze in less than an hour, and the ship returned to the line on March 30.

The deck of an aircraft carrier in combat, populated by airplanes loaded with jet fuel and armed with rocket-powered missiles and a wide variety of high explosives, is a tinderbox. A spark from either friendly or enemy hands can start an inferno.

Mishaps, rather than hostile action, have caused all carrier fires since World War II. Three of the most serious—aboard the *Oriskany* in 1966, the *Forrestal* in 1967, and the *Enterprise* in 1969—broke out during operations off the coast of Vietnam.

The *Forrestal* fire was the worst of the three. It began when one of the fifty-seven fighters and attack aircraft that were awaiting launch on the morning of July 29 accidentally fired a Zuni air-to-ground rocket. It flashed across the carrier and hit the drop tank of a fully fueled A-4 Skyhawk, spilling blazing JP-5 onto the flight deck.

As pilots leaped from their airplanes and sailors ran to man fire hoses, brisk winds swept the liquid aft. Flames soon licked at the bellies of several airplanes, some of which were carrying 1,000-pound bombs. In minutes, the bombs started to cook off, spreading fire in every direction and cutting down the nearest firefighters in hails of deadly shrapnel.

After each blast, more sailors came forward to pick up the hoses that had been dropped by their dead mates. Straddling their bodies, the men sprayed water on unexploded munitions to cool them while other sailors wrestled bombs, rockets, and fuel tanks over the side of the ship.

With assistance from nearby ships, the crew of the *Forrestal* succeeded in smothering the worst blazes with chemical foam by early afternoon, but they were still fighting sporadic reflashes at sunrise the next day. By that time, sixty-four planes, about 75 percent of the *Forrestal*'s air wing, had been damaged or destroyed, and 134 crewmen had lost their lives.

A Navy panel investigating the disaster found much to criticize: inadequate fire protection for the flight deck, unsafe fuel systems in the aircraft, and confusing weapons-handling procedures. But the panel most sharply criticized the lack of damage-control training on most aircraft carriers—something Captain Kent L. Lee, skipper of the *Enterprise*, took to heart.

Before the carrier's 1969 tour off the coast of North Vietnam, Lee sent his flight-deck crews, squadron maintenance personnel, and others to firefighting school. Then, during the voyage west, he took the additional step of ordering daily general-quarters drills. "We may have looked silly doing them every day for no apparent reason," recalled an *Enterprise* crew member, but when the carrier erupted in flames on January 14 *(left)*, "we knew what to do and where everything was because we had done it so many times before."

battle group. In one thirty-six-hour period, radar logged no fewer than seventy contacts, and the *Kitty Hawk*'s air group prosecuted every one. Few Soviet aircraft got within 200 miles of the carrier without finding Tomcats sitting on their wings.

The Soviet submarine in the drama—a 308-foot nuclear-powered Victor I attack boat—was a different, and possibly more dangerous, opponent. Ultimately, the sub would be at fault in one of the most bizarre encounters in the annals of U.S.-Soviet naval relations.

Ordinarily, a carrier's retinue includes several nuclear attack submarines, whose role is to stalk and kill an enemy sub before it can approach the carrier. Naval sources maintain that in this case, no U.S. subs participated. First contact with the Victor came from a land-based PC-3 Orion antisub patrol plane. Sent to sanitize the exercise area, it spotted the sub on the surface. Identifiable by its low, rounded conning tower, or sail, the Victor had surfaced 150 miles from the *Kitty Hawk*. In short order, the battle group brought its antisubmarine warfare (ASW) resources to bear.

First into action went the *Kitty Hawk*'s S-3A Vikings, big twin-jet subhunters and general-purpose aircraft, ten of which are included in a carrier air wing. Standard practice is to launch a pair of Vikings as soon as the carrier reaches its area of operations. Once aloft, each snub-nosed S-3 climbs to 20,000 feet or so and strikes out at 350 knots along a suspected or potential threat axis. Then, anywhere from 100 to 300 miles from the carrier, the Viking descends to low level and the systems operator starts dispensing acoustic sensors— yard-long cylindrical sonobuoys—from an array of circular tubes in the belly of the aircraft.

Relatively simple omnidirectional listening devices called Jezebels—each essentially an underwater microphone hooked to a floating radio transmitting on its own frequency—are usually the first into the water. An S-3 on a sub hunt will lay a number of these sonobuoys several miles apart in a grid or chevron pattern stretching across the threat axis. Then the plane loiters high overhead, listening for the sonobuoys to pick up the sound of a submarine. By comparing the loudness of the sound as reported by several of the sonobuoys, computers aboard the plane can calculate a rough position for the contact.

Next, the Viking swoops to low altitude and starts working to pinpoint the contact. Now the systems operator dispenses pinging sonobuoys in an area judged by computer to almost certainly contain the enemy sub. By comparing the times required by an echo to return to three or more sonobuoys, the computer further refines the location. With this information, the S-3 drops a tighter pattern of sonobuoys and so on, gradually isolating the contact to an area the size of a football field. In the final stages of the hunt, the Viking will descend to 500 feet and bring into play its magnetic anomaly detector (MAD)—a device that senses the minuscule deviations that submarines cause in the earth's magnetic field—and will drop a very tight pattern of loudly pinging sonobuoys. The game ends with the release of one—or all four—of the Mark 46 antisubmarine torpedoes in the Viking's internal bomb bay. Eight and a half feet long and weighing 568 pounds, the torpedo parachutes into the water then streaks at forty knots to the target, guiding itself by sonar. In this encounter with this Victor, naturally, the *Kitty Hawk*'s Vikings would drop no torpedoes.

The sub closed repeatedly on the carrier as five of the battle group's warships joined the defense: the guided-missile cruiser *Long Beach*; two guided-missile destroyers, the *Chandler* and the *Berkeley*; and two frigates, the guided-missile frigate *Lewis B. Puller* and the ASW frigate *Harold E. Holt*. While the *Long Beach* and the *Chandler* watched the skies, the *Puller*, the *Berkeley*, and the *Holt* dogged the submarine, monitoring the progress of the S-3s and pinging for the interloper themselves with active sonar. For destroying such a threat, the ships had ASROC, rocket-propelled Mark 46 torpedoes similar to those aboard the Vikings.

Yet along with the Vikings, the battle group's principal sub-killing weapons were—and remain—its helicopters: six big SH-3 Sea Kings on the *Kitty Hawk*, and one, sometimes two, smaller SH-2 or SH-60 LAMPS (light airborne multipurpose system) helos on each of the destroyers and frigates. Both the Sea Kings and LAMPS are equipped with radar, MAD gear, passive sonobuoys, and active, pinging sonar that can be lowered into the sea by cable from the hovering helicopters. Ranging out as far as 100 miles, a pair of torpedo-armed LAMPS can remain on station for an hour or longer, dipping their sonar and leapfrogging each other as they track a submerged submarine.

Undeterred by the cacophony of pinging sonar, the Victor's captain conned his sub right in among the battle group, trying to hide under vessels and in their wakes, where the helos had difficulty finding him. To distract the hunters, he occasionally launched decoys—small underwater vehicles with noisemakers that imitate the sounds of submarines—and fired bubbles of air or material that fizzes like Alka-Seltzer to confuse the American sonar. From time to time, the submarine would succeed in eluding its pursuers, and in a shooting war, it might have torpedoed the carrier. More likely, however, the Victor would have been sunk earlier. The Navy reported "killing" it at least thirteen times during three days' action.

Twice the Victor broached in the middle of the formation, exposing its sail so close aboard that the *Long Beach* and the *Puller* had to turn sharply to avoid ramming. Perplexed U.S. Navy men wondered if the Soviet captain had trouble controlling his depth—or if he simply felt like thumbing his nose at the Americans.

As the exercise with the Koreans entered a new stage, the battle group broke contact with the pesky Victor and ran south toward Tsushima Strait at high speed. Shortly after 10:00 p.m. on March 21, as the *Kitty Hawk* approached a replenishment point, she quickly slowed from twenty-five knots to fifteen, matching speed with the oiler *Wabash*.

At the time, the battle group commander, who customarily uses the carrier as his flagship, was sitting in his cabin reading a message when he felt the huge vessel shudder. "It seemed like a big wave slap," he recalled. "You get these large waves that will hit and you'll feel the ship jerk." He phoned the *Kitty Hawk*'s skipper, Captain David Rogers, on the bridge: "What the hell was that?"

It was the Victor.

An SH-3H Sea King carrier-based antisubmarine helicopter prepares to winch down a dipping sonar while a smoke flare burns in the distance. Departing helicopter crews often drop such flares as they leave the scene, marking the spot of last contact with the enemy submarine for another chopper coming to continue the pursuit.

Up on deck, an astonished lookout reported the black conning tower of the sub rolling violently back and forth as it slid along the starboard flank of the carrier, spouting geysers of mist from its ballast tanks. In a moment, the Victor had slipped astern, wallowing dead in the water and showing no lights. Rogers immediately ordered "all stop" and launched helicopters to find the stricken sub and to rescue any Soviet sailors who might have fallen into the sea.

No one may ever learn the reason for the collision, but this explanation seems consistent with events: Chasing the U.S. carrier at up to thirty knots, the Victor made so much noise that it failed to detect the *Kitty Hawk* slowing for its rendezvous. The sub overshot. A few moments later, bewildered at finding nothing ahead, the sub's skipper hurriedly surfaced for a look around, neglecting—as all good submariners must—to clear his baffles, that is, turn right and left to see what might be in the acoustic blind spot directly behind the submarine's propeller. "It was like a guy in a Volkswagen coming onto the autobahn without checking his rear-view mirror," said one participant.

Coming up behind, the *Kitty Hawk* hit the Victor a glancing blow on the starboard side near the stern, momentarily driving the 5,100-ton sub beneath the waves. Then it bobbed to the surface. Except for a fractured propeller—divers later found a two-foot-by-three-foot chunk of it embedded in the carrier's keel—and the resulting likelihood of a broken drive shaft, damage seemed to be minor. Within a few hours, the cruiser *Petropavlovsk* arrived on the scene. A tug eventually towed the crippled submarine to Vladivostok.

With rapprochement between the republics of the former Soviet Union and the United States, the prospect that the carrier battle group's multilayered defenses will ever be challenged by any foe even remotely capable of overwhelming them seems to recede as steadily as the calendar advances. Even so, Soviet submarines will no doubt continue to stalk American carriers when they can find them, if for no other reason than to keep up with any new tactics and weapons that America might devise to protect its flattops. And the battle group will prosecute the contacts, just as the F-14s have no choice but react to any approaching aircraft. After all, no flattop skipper wants to be the victim of a surprise like the one that nearly sank the *Stark*, even if it all turns out to be a big mistake. ★

Flight Ops: A Marvel of Precision Teamwork

No staging ground for combat demands more of those who perform there than the carrier flight deck, where 70,000-pound jets trailing fire are slung into the sky by steam-driven catapults and slam back down onto a landing area less than 800 feet long to snatch a slender steel cable and lurch to a stop. Like competitors in hostile confines, the flight-deck personnel who rule over these hectic comings and goings must carry on in the face of a mind-boggling din—screaming turbine engines that drown out all spoken words, forcing team members to rely on an elaborate repertoire of hand signals. And the cost of the slightest error can be steep indeed. A sailor on the flight deck who allows his attention to wander can be sucked into a jet-engine intake, tossed overboard by a blast of hot exhaust, or maimed by a snapped cable.

For the flight-deck crew, as for any successful team, faithful execution of a complex game plan under pressure requires a clear division of responsibilities. The role of each player in the overall scheme is signaled by the color of the shirt or vest he wears—yellow for the plane directors, the traffic cops of the flight deck; blue for the aircraft handlers, who mainly haul jets from the hangar deck to the flight deck and back with low-slung tractors; green for squadron maintenance personnel as well as the catapult and arresting gear crews, who manage the machinery of launch and recovery; brown for the plane captains, who see that each aircraft is properly serviced and secured to the deck with chains between flights; purple for the "grapes," or refuelers; red for firefighters and ordnance handlers; white for safety monitors; a black-and-white checkerboard pattern for troubleshooters and inspectors; and a red cross on white for medical personnel.

Calling the shots for the entire crew from the ship's island is the air boss, perched high above the deck in a control room. Like a coach and his staff on game day, the air boss and his assistants must cope with the many unpredictable circumstances that arise during flight operations, when the carefully rehearsed routine is tested against reality. At peak activity, the commotion on the deck may resemble a free-for-all, but in fact flight-deck hands' movements embody the ultimate in teamwork—the ability to respond quickly and correctly to any contingency.

Aboard the USS *Midway*, F/A-18 Hornet No. 106 waits behind an A-6 Intruder for its turn to take off from catapult No. 1, as another Hornet thunders down cat 2. The barrier behind the A-6 is a water-cooled jet-blast deflector; it will be lowered after the plane departs, permitting No. 106 to taxi into position over the catapult.

Managing the Flight Deck

Primary Flight Control, aerie of the yellow-jerseyed air boss, commands a view of the entire flight deck. From this glassed-in observation post, known as Pri-Fly, he and his assistant, the mini boss, supervise all activities on the flight deck and in the air within a ten-mile radius of the ship. An experienced naval aviator in his own right, the air boss makes sure that all conditions have been met for safe takeoffs and touchdowns. He frequently issues curt reminders and reprimands over the ship's PA system and through the earphones of busy flight-deck personnel, who know that lives depend on his stern vigilance.

While scrutinizing the deck from his vantage point, the air boss confers regularly with officers throughout the ship. He asks the captain's permission to proceed with launches and recoveries and consults the navigator to ensure that the carrier will be properly positioned to afford the jets enough headwind for takeoff. Periodically, he speaks with the carrier's chief engineer to confirm an adequate supply of steam for the catapults and of electricity for other vital gear.

To keep traffic flowing smoothly on the flight deck, the air boss and his second-in-command rely heavily on an assistant called the aircraft handling officer—or handler, for short. He monitors the status and location of every plane aboard. Stationed at a table where models of the aircraft sit on grids representing the flight deck and hangar deck, the handler ponders each move of an aircraft like a chess master. He confers constantly with crew supervisors who bombard him with reports and requests, weighs the possible impact of mechanical snags and other unforeseen developments, and decides where aircraft should be spotted next to make the most of limited space and clear the way for the next round of launches or landings. So complex are the handler's considerations that every attempt at programming a computer to do his job have failed.

Job titles stenciled on their yellow jerseys, the *Midway*'s air boss and mini boss keep a sharp eye on the flight deck and environs from Pri-Fly. Their high-tech crow's-nest is packed with a variety of gear, including communications equipment, weather gauges, and dials indicating the approach speed of aircraft preparing to land.

Fielding two calls at once, the handler works at his table, called the Ouija board. As detailed in the closeup below, numbered tapes and colored tails on the aircraft models indicate their squadron, while lettered disks and other tokens reveal their flight status. The PMCF disk atop the model of an A-6 Intruder, for example, tells the handler that the plane is ready for a post-maintenance check flight.

Heeding the command of the air boss, all hands on deck—including aircrews—form a line to search for debris that might be vacuumed up by a jet-engine intake or shot across the deck by a blast of exhaust. Called a FOD (foreign-object damage) walk-down, the task is taken most seriously; an item as small as a screw can destroy a turbine engine or lacerate a crewman.

A Quick Turnaround

The moment an incoming plane hooks an arresting cable and shudders to a halt, the multihued vests on the flight deck begin the complex process that readies the aircraft for its next flight. At a signal from a yellow-shirted plane director, the pilot raises his tailhook to free the cable, folds his wings, and taxis to his assigned tie-down spot, normally located near the bow of the carrier to keep the landing area clear until all aircraft aloft have been safely recovered. At the tie-down spot, another plane director signals the pilot to apply the brakes until the blue-shirted aircraft handlers, aided by the plane captain in brown, chock the wheels and chain the aircraft to the deck.

Once the aircrew has climbed out of the aircraft, the plane captain takes charge. Under his watchful eye, grapes in purple refuel the aircraft while "ordies"—ordnancemen wearing red—either remove the unused ammunition or, if the plane is slated for another mission soon, replenish its stock as required. The plane captain is responsible for checking fluid levels, examining the tires for wear or cuts, and cleaning the canopy. He also sees that any problem reported by the aircrew gets attention from the green-shirted maintenance personnel, who determine whether repairs can be handled in a short time on the flight deck or send the airplane by elevator to the hangar deck below.

After the carrier completes a landing sequence, airworthy planes are moved aft by a tractor. A blue shirt, directed by a yellow shirt, drives the tractor, while the plane captain rides in the cockpit to work the brakes. Transferring the aircraft to the rear of the flight deck readies the carrier to launch its jets from the bow catapults. Typically, a plane remains chocked and chained to its new tie-down spot, called the go spot, until the launch sequence begins.

A grape drags a refueling hose toward a chocked and chained A-7 Corsair. Once the hose is connected to the aircraft, aviation fuel will flow from the carrier's storage cells, where millions of gallons are on tap. Grapes also pump fuel from planes that are headed for the hangar deck.

Red-shirted ordies—who can mount ordnance weighing up to a half-ton without resorting to hydraulic lifts—attach a 500-pound bomb to the pylon of an A-6 Intruder. They are hoisting the bomb with "hernia bars" that screw into fuze wells in the weapon's nose and tail. After hanging the bomb, the ordies replace the bars with fuzes equipped with multiple safety devices to prevent the ordnance from detonating until after re-lease over the target.

Blue shirts stand by with chocks and chains, ready to secure a freshly fueled A-6 tanker that has been pulled by tractor to its go spot. The plane director in charge of the move can be seen showing clenched fists to the plane captain in the cockpit—the signal to apply the brakes until the aircraft is tied down. At far left, the assistant plane captain carries an oil bowser to service the engines.

A Methodical Start-up

To get a bird into the air from its go spot can take up to thirty minutes. The process begins with a walkaround inspection of the aircraft in which the plane captain and the aircrew, having suited up and attended their prelaunch briefing, walk slowly around the plane. The aircrew examines every surface, checks the landing gear, and makes certain that all of the aircraft's weapons are securely mounted.

Once the plane captain and the aircrew are satisfied that everything is in order, the aviators climb into the cockpit, where the plane captain and his assistant help to strap them into their ejection seats, plug in their helmet communications wires, and connect their oxygen hoses. Then, the fliers remove red-flagged safety pins from the firing mechanisms of their ejection seats and hand the pins to the brown shirts, and the brown shirts climb down to the flight deck for engine start.

With the exception of the self-starting F/A-18 Hornets, jet aircraft that fly from American aircraft carriers have engines that need a boost to get going. The plane captain, aided by blue-shirted aircraft handlers, hooks up an external electric supply cable to the jet and attaches a so-called huffer hose that injects air to spin the engine's turbine fast enough for the engine to run on its own.

When the engines are running, the cable and huffer are disconnected, and the plane captain passes control to a yellow shirt—a plane director—who signals for the removal of chocks and chains, motions the pilot to taxi the jet out of its slot, and starts him toward the catapult. En route, a succession of yellow shirts hand off the plane from one to the next while the brown shirts accompany the plane all the way to the catapult.

Moments before start-up, a brown-vested plane captain and his assistant make the final adjustments for the pilot of an F-14 Tomcat and his radar intercept officer in the backseat.

A plane captain signals a Prowler pilot to open an internal valve that allows hot air, ducted from a huffer, to spin the starboard engine's turbine at starting speed. Electricity to operate the valve and other aircraft systems comes by cable from the yellow cart next to the huffer. Blue shirts operate the two carts, while maintenance men wearing green stand by in case of mechanical problems.

Below, a plane director standing near the folded wing of an A6-E configured as a tanker extends his arm as he hands off the plane to the catapult spotter *(fore-ground)*, who accepts the transfer by raising his palm. The green shirt in the picture, a member of the catapult crew, will hook up the plane when it reaches the proper position on the cat track.

Countdown to Takeoff

A plane awaits its turn on the catapult behind a jet-blast deflector. When the preceding aircraft has cleared the deck, the deflector is lowered and the cat spotter guides the plane slowly forward, aligning its nosewheel with the track. While the pilot is inching the craft ahead, he uses hand signals to verify the weight of the loaded plane, as calculated in advance and displayed to him on a weight board. If a last-minute change in ordnance or fuel level has altered that figure by as little as a thousand pounds, the pilot gestures to that effect, and the information is relayed to the catapult room below-decks where catapult force is regulated. Too little force for the plane's weight, and the aircraft will fail to reach flying speed and will plunge into the sea; too much force can cause the catapult to overrun its track, disabling it.

Just before launch, a green-shirted hookup man sees that a launch bar, part of the plane's nosewheel strut, is linked to the catapult shuttle in the deck just ahead of the wheel; the launch bar disengages from the shuttle on takeoff. A holdback bar, projecting behind the nosewheel strut to a slot in the deck, restrains the aircraft when the pilot applies power before launch. The holdback bar attaches to the strut by a spring-loaded clip that snaps open when the catapult is fired, releasing the aircraft for its takeoff roll.

When the plane is ready to go, the cat spotter signals a green shirt called the deck-edge operator—triggerman for the catapult—to apply enough steam pressure to the device to put tension on the shuttle. At this point, the pilot advances throttles to maximum power without afterburners.

Control now passes to the cat officer, or shooter. He waits until checkered-shirted troubleshooters—checkers, for short—have scrutinized the aircraft and given a thumbs-up. Raising his arm and opening his hand, the cat officer signals the pilot to go to afterburners (if his aircraft has them), holding that position until the checkers reply in kind to confirm that the tailpipe nozzles are open and the burners lit.

Bracing for launch, the pilot salutes the cat officer, who echoes the motion. With a final flourish, the shooter drops to one knee and lowers his hand to the deck, then raises it. At this, the deck-edge operator presses a button to fire the device. The clip in the holdback bar releases, and the jet screams down the flight deck into the sky.

Wreathed in steam venting from the catapult, the cat spotter stands astride the track and aligns an F-14 Tomcat to the satisfaction of another yellow shirt, the cat safety observer. Left of the fighter, the green-shirted hookup man waits to attach the holdback bar, while a checker behind the right wing makes a final inspection of the Tomcat's control surfaces.

After checking the takeoff weight of an A-6 Intruder with the pilot, the weight-board operator displays the figure—54,000 pounds—to the catapult officer (standing to the right of a trainee) and to the center deck operator (seated in hatch). Armed with the temperature and wind speed, the center deck operator consults a manual for the proper catapult setting for the weight. Upon confirmation by the shooter, the setting is called to the catapult control room deep within the ship.

s the hookup man crouches ongside an F/A-18 Hornet, the creeps forward, nudging its unch bar up the incline of the catapult shuttle to engage a notch in its forward end. The holdback bar can be seen behind the strut.

The hookup man sprints away from an F-14, his thumb raised to signal the cat spotter that the launch- and holdback-bar connections are secure. With the jet-blast deflector raised behind the plane, launch is no more than twenty seconds away.

Flames shoot from the exhaust nozzles of an F-14 as the cat officer, standing at far right, opens his hand, telling the pilot to light afterburners. Near the cat officer stands the deck-edge operator, both arms elevated to announce that his control panel is ready to fire the catapult. Checkers at the Tomcat's tail offer thumbs-up, signaling that the afterburners are lit and operating normally.

Every curve in the cat officer's body says "Go!" as he cues the deck-edge operator to fire the catapult *(above)*. Under the combined impetus of the steam-driven shuttle and its own roaring engines, the jet hurtles skyward hardly more than two seconds after it begins rolling.

Birds on a Wire

Carrier pilots once relied completely on a landing signal officer (LSO) to get safely down on deck. Stationed near the stern of the ship, the LSO used a pair of paddles and body language to keep a pilot on the glide path, the imaginary line that leads to the optimum touchdown point. Today a system of lenses and lights—called the Fresnel lens optical landing system (FLOLS)—has largely taken over the job of guiding pilots to safe landings.

Largely, but not entirely. At night, for example, the LSO, able to see the plane's navigation lights, is a better judge of altitude than the pilot. Rough seas that can pitch the rear of the flight deck twenty feet above the horizon, then down forty feet render the FLOLS useless. In these circumstances, the LSO again becomes the flier's guardian angel. He must judge whether an approaching aircraft will land safely or must be waved off for another try. A seasoned carrier pilot, the LSO weighs such variables as wind direction, visibility, deck motion, and aircraft characteristics to make the crucial call.

In daylight and fair weather, the LSO's duties are more routine. He and his backup—a supervisor with override authority—occupy a platform jutting from the port side aft of the arresting cables where they have a closeup view of incoming jets, yet remain clear of the landing area. When a plane is within three-quarters of a mile, the LSO takes control of the flight from the air boss, who has already identified the aircraft and passed its weight to arresting-engine crews belowdecks who set the machinery to the proper resistance.

Both the LSO and his backup grip pickle switches that control flashing red wave-off lights mounted on the FLOLS. Either officer may turn on the lights for a number of reasons. An aircraft within seconds of touchdown may be flying too fast or have wandered too far from the glide path. Or a plane may be slow in taxiing from the landing area, forcing the LSO to wave off the next in line. A pilot given a wave-off must add power and go around for another try.

Not the least of the LSO's duties is to grade each landing. In this role, he may seem to pilots more adversary than helpmate, but the purpose is to keep aircrews sharp, for their own and the ship's safety.

Below, an LSO and his backup maintain radio contact with an approaching pilot while holding their pickle switches aloft. The signal matches red deck-status lights on the FLOLS indicating that the deck is not clear for landing. When the lights turn green, the two LSOs lower their arms, ready to issue a wave-off if it is needed. As soon as five seconds later, the plane slams to the deck beside them.

At right, an F-14 Tomcat, tailhook down, whines past the LSO platform *(top)*. A heartbeat later, the hook snags a wire *(middle)*, which pays out at a rate calculated to stop the plane quickly, but without damage—typically within 350 feet of impact. After the aircraft stops, the cable slackens for the green shirts, seen advancing toward the jet in the bottom picture, to free it from the tailhook and reset it for the next landing.

Showdown in the South Atlantic

Raising clouds of spray from a wet flight deck, a Sea Harrier lifts off the aircraft carrier *Hermes*'s ski-jump ramp, assigned to dawn patrol over the Falkland Islands in May 1982. The Navy planes scored all the air-combat victories of the Falklands War, while nearly identical Royal Air Force Harriers *(foreground)* performed reconnaissance and ground-attack missions.

It was a situation to provoke nightmares in a British sea lord. On April 2, 1982, after 150 years of rancorous dispute with Great Britain over ownership of the Falkland Islands, Argentina had brought the matter to a head by forcibly seizing those barren flyspecks in the wind-blasted South Atlantic. Britain thundered in monumental outrage, but the Argentines had every reason to believe that their bold action would succeed. For starters, the Falklands lay 8,000 miles from the United Kingdom and held no value for the British, either economic or strategic. Furthermore, the seizure had caught the once-vaunted British armed forces woefully short. In particular, the Royal Navy, after years of budgetary cheeseparing, had become a mere shadow of the mighty establishment that had for centuries ruled the waves.

No matter, war it would be, with whatever meager assets could be scraped together. Besides a substantial number of troops, a victory would depend on air power to protect the soldiers ashore and the vessels that brought them from air attack. Yet for aircraft carriers, the British could summon up only the elderly 28,700-ton *Hermes* and the still smaller 19,500-ton *Invincible.* Both carried the same official designation: antisubmarine warfare vessel.

To launch from the *Hermes*'s and the *Invincible*'s flight decks, postage-stamp size by American standards, the Royal Navy had only a curious-looking subsonic fighter-bomber originally developed for the Royal Air Force and only recently operational in a seagoing role. Named the Sea Harrier, it was the latest in a lineage called V/STOL aircraft, for vertical/short takeoff and landing. Jet engine exhausts of both the RAF and the Royal Navy versions could be rotated to direct, or vector, thrust at any angle between directly rearward and straight down. With this capability, a Harrier could hover like a helicopter on its jet blast, then make a transition to

640-knot conventional flight or exploit any regime in between. No Harrier had ever faced combat, and in any case, the Navy owned only thirty-two of the planes. Of those, only twenty would initially be available for the fight.

Instead of catapults to launch the so-called jump jets, the flight decks of the *Hermes* and the *Invincible* ended in ramps that had the effect of tossing the aircraft aloft. By aiming thrust partly downward, a Harrier pilot could take off from the ramp at half the speed in one-third the distance he would need on a conventional runway with all the thrust directed to the rear. In addition to short takeoffs, vectored thrust permitted the Harriers to work either in mirror calm or in a gale that would leave the pilots on flat-deck carriers languishing in their ready rooms. Launching from such ships is possible in heavy seas if catapult shots are timed to coincide with the pitching bow as it rises above the horizon. However, trying to land in weather so foul would risk smashing into the stern.

By contrast, a Harrier could sidle toward the relatively stable center of a heaving deck and set down without incident. Superbly nimble, especially at the low altitudes where most of the combat would take place, the little Harriers had a weapons advantage over the Argentines: the all-aspect AIM-9L Sidewinder. This air-to-air missile can home on a jet's hot exhaust from any angle, not just the rear, a feature that permits firing the weapon at an attacker approaching head-on.

For the impending conflict, the *Hermes* and the *Invincible* would be operating with their pitiably few planes nearly 4,000 miles from the nearest British base at Ascension Island. Against them—and working within 500 miles of their homeland—would be Latin America's second-largest navy and an air force with an arsenal of 120 warplanes, including supersonic French-built Mirage III fighters, equally swift Dagger fighter-bombers derived from the Mirage,

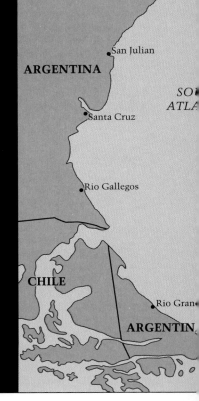

This map shows the 200-mile total exclusion zone *(circle)* established by British forces around the Falkland Islands on April 30 as a security measure; any Argentine forces entering the zone risked attack without warning. To defend against air raids, Sea Harriers took up stations west of the islands and at both ends of Falkland Sound to intercept Argentine planes approaching from mainland bases. Reaching these positions required the jets to fly more than 200 miles from their carriers *(blue rectangles)*, which sailed well east of the conflict to reduce the risk of air attack.

sturdy U.S.-supplied A-4 Skyhawk strikers that had proved their worth in Vietnam and in numerous violent encounters between Israel and its Arab neighbors, and French-made Super Etendards capable of carrying long-range Exocet antiship missiles.

Yet for all of that, on April 5, the two aircraft carriers, along with their escorts, resolutely shaped a course south for Ascension Island, and thence to the Falklands. There, as the world looked on in amazement, the small carriers and their peculiar aircraft would defeat everything the Argentines could hurl at them. In so doing, they would write a brilliant new chapter in the technology and conduct of naval aviation.

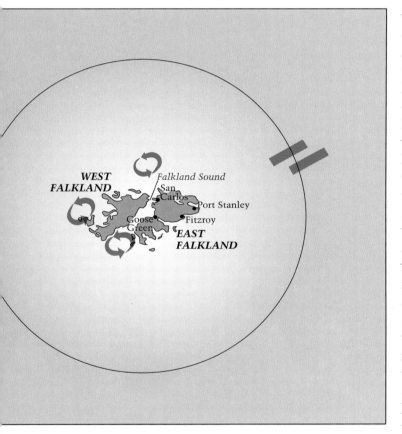

Flying in fog, rain, snow, sleet, and raging winds, the Royal Navy jump jets and their Royal Air Force counterparts, the Harrier GR3s, a handful of which arrived for the last three weeks of the war, would fly more than 2,000 sorties from the *Hermes* and the *Invincible*. As the guardians of surface ships and of British forces ashore, these planes would face as many as fifty Argentine raiders in a day, pilots who attacked with such skill and courage that the British would lose six ships sunk and another twelve damaged. Yet the Argentines would never achieve their main objective: to destroy the carriers and then savage the ground troops from the air. So superior would the Harriers and their pilots prove to be that they would destroy twenty-eight Argentine aircraft without a single loss in aerial combat. While some of the planes guarded the fleet, others would drop nearly 300 tons of ordnance in close support of troops on the ground.

Britain would win the war, and while no one could claim a single-handed victory for the Fleet Air Arm of the Royal Navy, without air support, the deployment of a fleet so close to the enemy mainland would have been a suicidal gesture. Britain's first sea lord, Admiral Sir Henry Leach, put it clearly. "Without the Sea Harrier," he said, "there could have been no task force."

The air war in the Falklands opened at 4:46 a.m. on May 1, when a lone RAF Vulcan heavy bomber, flying from Ascension Island and refueled en route by eleven aerial tankers, appeared over the Falklands' capital, Port Stanley, and laid a string of twenty-one 1,000-pound bombs across the airfield there. With this long-range raid, Britain intended to convey the idea that Vulcans could as easily bomb Buenos Aires, thereby causing the Argentines to divert a significant part of their air force to mainland defense. Argentina would indeed hold back most of its top-line Mirage fighters, perhaps as much from reluctance to challenge the Sea Harriers in air-to-air combat as from the psychological impact of the May Day attack. As for the airfield, only one of the bombs cratered the runway. On balance, the mission served primarily to rouse the Falklands' Argentine defenders for the real business to follow: a coordinated low-level attack by nine Sea Harriers to rain cluster bombs over the buildings, the fuel dump, and any aircraft parked on the tarmac.

On the evening of April 30, lead elements of the carrier task force had crossed the invisible circle the British had drawn 200 miles around the Falklands—an exclusion zone in which all Argentine sea and air traffic was prohibited. First light on May 1 found the British fleet less than 100 miles northeast of Port Stanley. From the *Invincible*, a flight of six Sea Harriers, each carrying two Sidewinders and a full magazine of 30-mm cannon ammunition, took position at 15,000 feet and 100 miles west of the fleet to serve as combat air patrol (CAP) against any probing Argentine aircraft. Meanwhile, Lieutenant Commander Andy Auld, commanding officer of 800 Naval Air Squadron aboard the *Hermes*, shoved his throttle to its forward stop and, propelled by 21,500 pounds of thrust, accelerated toward the end of the 12-degree ramp 600 feet away. In rapid succession, eleven other bomb-laden Sea Harriers followed, racing southwest toward the Falklands a mere fifty feet above the swells. At about 8:00 a.m., three of the planes broke off and headed toward an Argentine-held airfield at Goose Green, a settlement near the beaches that had been selected for amphibious landings.

Four Sea Harriers would lead the attack on Port Stanley airfield. They would fly at 100 feet and 520 knots to a point three miles from the target, where the pilots would pull up into a 30-degree climb and loft three 1,000-pound iron bombs apiece in a maneuver that one of the pilots later compared to "an underarm cricket-ball delivery." While the Harriers turned away, the bombs would arc toward the target for about twenty seconds before being triggered by radar altimeter fuses to explode in the air, suppressing fire from Argentine gun and missile positions. "If you've got things blowing up around people's heads," explained Flight Lieutenant Dave Morgan, a Royal Air Force pilot assigned to the Navy and a participant in the mission, "they hit the dirt." Before the defenders could recover, four of the remaining five Sea Harriers would come howling in with cluster bombs. The fifth would carry three more half-tonners.

"That was the plan," Morgan said later. "But as with most plans, the thing gets a little screwed up." So that they would not blunder into a sheet of flying metal from the bombs of the first group, the cluster bombers intended to orbit a speck of land called Cochon Island just offshore until they got a "bombs-gone" message from the last of the toss bombers.

"Everything went fine," recalled Morgan, flying as wingman to the leader of the cluster bombers, Andy Auld. "We were just ap-

Plowing through rough seas, the carrier *Hermes,* flagship for Britain's effort to retake the Falklands, heads toward the war zone. Alongside steams the frigate *Broadsword,* the carrier's "goalkeeper" and one of just two task force men-of-war equipped with Sea Wolf missiles to provide close-range point defense for the *Hermes* and the *Invincible,* the second carrier sent to the South Atlantic.

proaching the island when I heard 'bombs gone.' At this stage, Andy Auld unfortunately had a partial radio failure and didn't hear the call. So he started his 360-degree turn, and me being a good number two stuck with him.''

Until then, Morgan had felt reasonably safe: ''I'd worked out that the safest place for Mrs. Morgan's little lad was number two over the target. They might shoot the leader down because he was going in first. They may well shoot the last guy down because by that time they'd be pretty mad. But number two should get away with it.''

Now, as he circled with his leader, Morgan was horrified to see that the other three Sea Harriers were already streaking toward the airfield in response to the bombs-gone message. Clearly, instead of being in the relatively comfortable second position, Morgan would now be in the most perilous place of all—dead last over the target.

In he went nonetheless. Swinging low and hard around a hill, he could see ahead ''sand dunes with people firing down at me from the top and bombs exploding and missiles going off everywhere. There was a complete umbrella of antiaircraft fire bursting all over the airfield.'' Instinct took over. ''Without me doing anything,'' he said, ''I saw my hand push forward and then pull back, and I was flying at about ten feet at about 480 knots.''

Just short of the airfield, Morgan climbed to about 150 feet—the minimum height for his cluster bombs to fuze before impact—and saw a Britten-Norman Islander light transport plane taxiing across the grass. ''Thinking, 'okay, you're the first one,' I pickled the first cluster bomb on him,'' Morgan recalled, ''and blew him away.'' Then, one-third of a second later, as Morgan released a second bomb, there was ''a great bloody explosion behind me and my aircraft started shaking violently.''

Since the Harrier was still flying, Morgan unloaded his third bomb directly on some buildings and started looking for an escape from the flak. ''There was a lovely bit of smoke where one of the guys ahead of me had hit the fuel dump,'' he recalled. ''I just shoved the stick forward and went into it from 100 feet. Ran out of this smoke at fifteen or twenty feet and I remember seeing this beautiful white sandy beach, with lovely blue sea and little white breakers on it and thinking it was quite nice. At that stage I was locked up by Skyguard radar, which I knew was tied into a lot of 35-mm antiaircraft guns that would have been a pretty nasty thing to collect.''

To confuse the radar, Morgan blipped open his speed brake, re-

As dawn breaks over the South Atlantic, Royal Marines line up for a weapons check on the *Hermes*'s brightly lighted hangar deck. In the background, Sea Harrier maintenance crews go over their planes with a thoroughness that would ensure, in the fighting to come, that virtually every one of the planes was serviceable at all times.

leased a bundle of chaff, pulled hard to his left, then reversed his turn to again point the nose of his plane east toward the *Hermes*. As he neared the carrier, another Sea Harrier pulled alongside him. "Ahhhh!" the pilot told Morgan. "There's a bloody great big hole in your tail and some damage down the side on the stabilizer."

Under ordinary circumstances, Morgan would have made a vertical landing by slowing the plane to 250 knots as he approached the carrier, then swiveling the engine's exhaust nozzles in stages to direct the thrust downward at a 90-degree angle, stabilizing the Harrier in a hover and plopping it straight down onto the flight deck. But Morgan worried now that the power required for a vertical landing would be too much for his damaged machine, so he kept enough forward speed to land with a little forward roll.

Safely down, Morgan found a fist-size shell hole in his tail fin—the only significant damage suffered in a raid in which the British had expected to lose two or three Sea Harriers. Within half an hour, the eleven still-operational Harriers had been serviced and readied to fend off with Sidewinders the attacks they knew were coming.

By the time Dave Morgan and his fellow Harrier pilots returned from their strike against the Port Stanley airfield, five British warships had detached themselves from the rest of the task force. The frigates *Brilliant* and *Yarmouth*, accompanied by Sea King helicopters from the *Hermes*, set off on an antisubmarine sweep twenty miles off the northeast coast of East Falkland, while the destroyer *Glamorgan*, along with the frigates *Arrow* and *Alacrity*, pushed within seven miles of Port Stanley. There, at about 1:30 p.m., they began bombarding coastal defense installations as if in preparation for a major landing of troops. The feint opened a series of ruses aimed at diverting Argentine attention from the actual site of the British invasion, still nearly three weeks away, on the opposite side of East Falkland, the larger of the two Falkland islands.

As expected, the Argentines reacted violently. Fully convinced that an assault was imminent, Air Force commanders on the mainland launched a maximum-effort antiship campaign. From four air bases in southern Argentina, they sent twenty-eight A-4 Skyhawks, a dozen Dagger fighter-bombers, six twin-engine Canberra medium bombers, and, flying in pairs as high-altitude escorts, ten of Argentina's prized Mirage IIIs.

A fighter controller on the *Glamorgan* spotted two of the incoming planes and vectored a pair of patrolling Harriers for the intercept. Acquiring the enemy aircraft on their radar, Flight Lieutenant Paul Barton, another RAF pilot, and Lieutenant Steve Thomas could hardly believe what they saw: Heading straight toward them at about 15,000 feet were two fighters in tight echelon with the wingman to the rear and left of the leader. In that awkward formation, the second plane could not fire a heat-seeking missile without risking that it run right up the leader's tailpipe. Furthermore, the leader was in no position to help his wingman against an enemy coming up from the rear. "This," said Barton, "is the sort of thing one learns not to do on day one at the Tactical Weapons Unit."

As Barton peeled off to swing around behind the Argentines, Thomas continued flying straight ahead. At eight miles, he identified the planes as Mirages; at five miles, both bandits fired missiles at him. They dribbled harmlessly away. Thomas, after trying without success to lock a Sidewinder onto one of the Mirages, broke hard right to cross 100 feet above the enemy leader. In that split second, said Thomas, "I could make out every detail of the aircraft, its camouflage pattern, and see the pilot in the cockpit."

By then, Barton had completed his flanking maneuver to come up behind the Argentine wingman. "If he had seen me, any red-blooded fighter pilot would have broken hard toward me as I turned in," Barton said later. "But he did nothing." As the growl of his starboard Sidewinder switched to a warble, signifying lock-on, Barton pressed the red firing button and the AIM-9 went off with a whooosh. "At first I thought it had failed," the pilot recalled. "It came off the rail and ducked down. It took about half a mile for it to get its trajectory sorted out, then it picked up and just homed straight in."

A couple of miles away, Barton's partner, Thomas, who had continued his attack on the enemy leader, saw the Sidewinder explode and the rear of the Mirage blossom into a bright yellow torch. He had little time to contemplate the victory, however, because his own opponent "was doing quite a hard descending turn to the left," said Thomas, "going down very fast towards the top of the solid cloud cover at 4,000 feet. I rolled into a vertical descent behind him, locked on one of my missiles and fired it. The missile streaked after him and just before it reached cloud I saw it pass close to his tail. Then both the aircraft and the missile vanished."

Later, the British would learn that Thomas's Sidewinder had exploded close to the Mirage, whose pilot afterward attempted an emergency landing at the Port Stanley airfield. Watching from his garden, a Falkland Islander saw the crippled Mirage coming in from the west. "Suddenly the Argentine guns opened up at it, everything they had in and around the town joined in the firing," said the Falklander. "They hit it once, twice, and down she came. She smashed into the ground and the Argentines cheered like a football crowd." Elation turned to grief, however, when they discovered that they had shot down one of their own planes, killing the pilot.

Of the fifty-six aircraft dispatched from the Argentine mainland, twenty had turned back with mechanical difficulties and fuel shortages. Of those that reached the Falklands, a Dagger and a Canberra fell to Harriers, in addition to the two Mirages. Only three enemy aircraft found targets, attacking the three ships bombarding Port Stanley and causing minor damage to all of them.

Interestingly, neither on this day nor on any later occasion was the Harrier called upon to perform its most celebrated maneuver: VIFFing (for vectoring in forward flight). By manipulating the plane's engine nozzles, a Harrier pilot can swiftly slow the aircraft from 600 to 200 knots or less, causing conventional fighters to overshoot and place themselves in the Harrier's sights. In similar fashion, a Harrier can roll inverted and virtually drop out of the sky to turn

An Argentine 20-mm shell punched this fist-size hole in the tail of the Sea Harrier flown by Dave Morgan *(left)* during a bombing mission against Port Stanley airfield on May 1. Mechanics applied a patch to the damage, and the jet was ready to rejoin the action before the end of the day.

the tables on an enemy or execute exceptionally tight turns to escape attack. Argentine fliers knew of the Harrier's VIFFing capability. "The important thing," said a Mirage pilot, "was not to try to follow the Sea Harriers for very long at low altitude, because the Mirage III can very quickly end up in front."

During the fighting in the Falklands, however, VIFFing never became necessary. "The problem with VIFFing," a Sea Harrier pilot explained, "is you lose energy. If you are in an attacking situation, you don't VIFF because you want to retain your energy. One of the best places to use VIFF is in a defensive maneuver. The reason you didn't see it in the Falklands is we were never put in a defensive situation." After those first losing encounters with the Harriers, Argentine commanders decided to forgo fighter escorts for their strikers. Henceforth, the bomb-laden Skyhawks and Daggers would be on their own to find their way through the Harrier patrols and the gun and missile defense put up by the British ships. The character of the air war in the Falklands was swiftly taking shape, but during the next three days, two more events would drastically affect carrier operations for the remainder of the conflict.

Since April 26, an Argentine fleet, built around the carrier *Veinticinco de Mayo*, had been at sea, making its way down from the northwest toward the Falklands. On May 1, its Tracker reconnaissance aircraft located the British task force only 180 miles east of the islands, and the Argentine carrier prepared to launch six A-4 Skyhawks against the *Hermes* and the *Invincible*. Setting the strike for dawn the next day, the Argentines envisioned another glorious Midway, the World War II battle in which an inferior American carrier force devastated a Japanese invasion fleet, thereby altering the course of the war. But the notoriously fickle South Atlantic weather was about to make a mockery of Argentine aspirations.

Burdened with three 500-pound bombs and fuel enough for the round trip, the Skyhawks would require about 125 knots airspeed to lift off the *Veinticinco de Mayo*'s conventional flight deck. Combined, the thirty-seven-year-old carrier's catapult and 24-knot speed could provide about 100 knots, but the rest would have to come from the wind, ordinarily blowing at 30 knots or more in those latitudes. Yet, as the hour for launch approached, a dead calm prevailed in the South Atlantic, forcing cancellation of the strike. Once

Crewmen aboard the Argentine aircraft carrier *Veinticinco de Mayo* ready an A-4 Skyhawk for a load of 500-pound bombs for an unrealized encounter with a high prize, the Royal Navy's HMS *Invincible.* This version of the bomb, called a Snakeye, has "petals" at the rear that open after release to slow the weapon. Without this feature, a bomber attacking at low level could be knocked down by the explosion of its own ordnance.

lost, the opportunity would never be regained, as events to the south were about to end the Argentine fleet's participation.

For several days, the Argentine heavy cruiser *General Belgrano* had been skirting the southern edge of the 200-mile exclusion zone around the Falklands. Shadowing the cruiser was the British nuclear attack submarine *Conqueror.* Since the *Belgrano* and its two escorting destroyers each carried a seagoing version of the Exocet missile, the British feared that they might bolt northward during the night, somehow shake the *Conqueror,* and get close enough to launch Exocets at the two carriers. To preempt any such calamity, the task force commander, Admiral John Woodward, ordered the *Conqueror* to attack. On the afternoon of May 2, the submarine put two Mark 8 torpedoes into the *General Belgrano,* which swiftly sank—taking with it 321 of the ship's company of 1,093.

The loss of the *General Belgrano* caused the *Veinticinco de Mayo* and the rest of the Argentine fleet to scurry for home waters, where the ships remained for the duration. Despite diplomatic and press protests against the British for having attacked a ship outside the exclusion zone, the Royal Navy offered no apology. Indeed, two days later, events would justify British concern about the Exocet.

From the very beginning of the Falklands crisis it had been clear that the British would have to operate without airborne early warn-

Giving the Harrier a Boost

A Sea Harrier vaults skyward from the ski-jump ramp of the aircraft carrier *Invincible*. The netting at the edge of the ramp is a safety measure for deck personnel working in high winds.

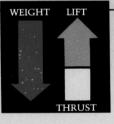

WEIGHT LIFT

THRUST

Faced with shrinking defense budgets and a diminishing military role in the world, the United Kingdom in 1966 canceled plans for HMS *Furious*, a modern new flattop. Future aircraft carriers of the Royal Navy would be smaller and cheaper, functioning as helicopter platforms for Britain's antisubmarine warfare (ASW) role within NATO. They would lack the catapults and arresting gear needed to launch and land fixed-wing aircraft. An era seemed to have passed.

But then, in 1970, a Royal Air Force pilot landed one of the new RAF Harrier V/STOL (vertical/short takeoff and landing) aircraft, supported by the exhaust of its vectored-thrust engine, straight down onto the deck of one of the Navy's helicopter carriers. The demonstration galvanized advocates of fixed-wing air power within the Navy Department; there seemed little reason not to adopt a plane that could take off and land like a chopper.

One obstacle stood in the way: Fuel consumed during a vertical takeoff so reduced the plane's payload and combat radius as to make the plane impractical. A short takeoff run along the flight deck economized on fuel, but more was needed. So the Navy curved the forward end of the deck upward to launch the planes on a climbing trajectory that further improved performance *(below).* Two such "ski-jump" ships were ready for the Falklands War: the *Hermes*, to which a ramp had been added, and the *Invincible*, built from the keel up as a floating base for Harriers.

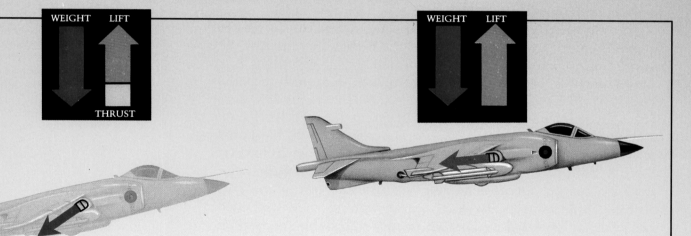

A Harrier launching from a ski-jump carrier passes through four stages on takeoff, during which thrust from the engine supports part of the plane's weight until the jet accelerates to a speed sufficient for the wings to generate the lift needed for flight. At far left, the Harrier reaches the threshold of the ramp after a short takeoff roll. Speed is 60 knots and exhaust nozzles point directly aft *(red arrow).* Less than a second later, the plane leaves the ramp at 80 knots, but with engine thrust rotated downward at 50 degrees. The lift from the wings and the vectored thrust from the engine combine to equal the weight of the plane. As it accelerates away from the ramp, it depends less on downward thrust and more on lift, so the nozzles are gradually adjusted in favor of forward speed. At 110 knots, flying speed, thrust is directed aft once more.

ing. Only U.S. Air Force E-3 airborne warning and control aircraft had the range to fly from Ascension Island, and the Royal Navy had nothing to compare with the U.S. Navy's carrier-based E-2C Hawkeye. Instead, the task force set up a radar picket line of destroyers and frigates about twenty miles west of the carriers and sent out Harriers to patrol the vast expanse of the South Atlantic that lay beyond. The screen was porous, and the Argentines knew it.

At about 7:00 on the morning of May 4, a Neptune reconnaissance plane belonging to the Argentine Navy reported radar contact with a group of ships eighty-five miles south of Port Stanley. Now the Argentines could proceed. Some months earlier, they had acquired five air-launched Exocet missiles as a partial order from France. Called the AM-39, the missile could skim six feet above the waves at 600 knots for a distance of up to forty-five miles.

Given the paucity of their Exocets, the Argentines had decided to reserve them for top-priority targets—the British carriers. On the assumption that the Neptune had located those very ships, two Super Etendards, each with an Exocet tucked under its starboard wing, took off from the air base at Río Grande at about 9:45 a.m. With a flight of some 500 miles ahead of them, the aircraft refueled from one of Argentina's two KC-130 Hercules tankers and bored eastward at medium altitude. At a distance of 130 miles from their objective, the pilots descended to 50 feet to slip under British radar. Fifty miles out, chancing detection, the pilots popped up to 2,000 feet for a three-second radar scan. Seeing nothing, they descended once again to low level for another twenty miles, then popped up and quickly down again. This time the radar showed two contacts, one of them much larger than the other. "We thought it was an aircraft carrier," one of the Argentine pilots said later.

They were mistaken; the big, bright radar echo was the destroyer *Sheffield*, one of the warships in the British carrier force's defensive picket line and about to suffer for its exposed position.

Now, only twenty miles from their target and comfortably within the AM-39's range, the Super Etendards eased up to 120 feet. Taking radar fixes on the larger contact, the Argentine pilots fed its bearing and range into the missile's computer system. "Launch!" radioed the flight leader, and off went the missiles.

One of the Exocets failed to track, but the other dipped to a height of six feet and raced straight toward the *Sheffield*, kept on course toward the ship it could not yet see with its own radar by an inertial guidance system. Six miles—a mere thirty-one seconds—from the destroyer, the Exocet's radar homing head took control, steering the missile toward the center of the radar image.

Argentine tactics worked perfectly. Although radar aboard British ships picked up the Super Etendards when they popped up briefly to show the target to the Exocets, the planes vanished from the scopes before the ships could lock on with Sea Dart antiaircraft missiles. The next sign of an attack came when two lieutenants on the destroyer's bridge saw a trail of smoke from the missile. Five seconds later, the Exocet slammed into the destroyer amidships and penetrated deep into its hull. Twenty British sailors died, and the mortally wounded *Sheffield* sank while under tow on May 10.

Losing a major combatant hurt, but even more chilling was the realization that the Super Etendards need have penetrated only a few miles farther to have launched their Exocets against the carriers themselves. From then on, the British commanders would hold the *Hermes* and the *Invincible* nearly 200 miles to the east of the Falklands, vastly complicating any Argentine attempt to mount an air attack. Critics derided such caution, but the commanders on the scene knew that if they lost the carriers, they would lose the war.

During the next two weeks, foul weather held air operations to a minimum. Planning continued, however, for the British amphibious landings scheduled for May 21 at San Carlos Water, an inlet on the west coast of East Falkland where Marines and paratroopers would go ashore. Reaching the inlet required sailing into Falkland Sound, a narrow passage between East and West Falkland.

As D-day approached, the problem of protecting the foot soldiers from air attack became apparent. With a round trip of 400 miles, a Sea Harrier might have fuel enough for as little as ten minutes' CAP over the beachhead. The arrival on May 18 of eight more Sea Harriers and six RAF GR3 ground-attack Harriers helped. There would be enough planes, one pilot explained, for each carrier to "have two aircraft on combat air patrol, two on their way out to relieve them, and two on their way back." Even with such a schedule, gaps in air cover for the troop landings would be inevitable. By even the most optimistic calculations, there would barely be enough aircraft to meet anticipated Argentine air attacks.

In the early-morning darkness of May 21, British troops began going ashore, unopposed. Seven warships sailed into Falkland Sound and arrayed themselves at the entrance to San Carlos Water,

Two sailors aboard HMS *Sheffield* battle fires that broke out when an air-launched Exocet missile struck the vessel on May 4 with—according to the ship's commander, Captain Sam Salt *(inset)*—a "short, sharp, unimpressive bang." After a four-hour fight to save the *Sheffield,* the crew abandoned the ship to the flames.

guardians for the men on the beach and the ships that brought them there. Starting at dawn, pairs of Sea Harriers alternated taking off for their CAP stations from the *Hermes* and the *Invincible*, and the entire British force braced for the air assault that was sure to come.

Enemy aircraft arrived from the mainland at 9:35 a.m., when a formation of six Daggers raced over West Falkland, burst through a gap in the hills, and made a slashing attack on the warships in Falkland Sound, which soon became known to the British as Bomb Alley and to the Argentines as Death Valley. As they would almost invariably do throughout the war, the attackers came in at wave-top level, below the gaze of British radar.

The Argentine pilots flew with an élan that earned the admiration of British aviators. "Any guy who can fly at sixty or seventy feet above the waves, picking his way between ships' masts, is a pretty skillful pilot," said Flight Lieutenant Barton. But the virtuoso performance also defeated itself: The attackers roared in so low that many 1,000-pound bombs did not have time to fuze properly.

Again and again throughout that fiery day, Argentine Skyhawks and Daggers assailed the warships. Forced to abandon their carefully laid plans for parceling out air cover, British carrier commanders increased the number of Harriers over Falkland Sound to as many as ten at a time. Arriving at their patrol position in the early afternoon, Lieutenant Commander Neil Thomas and Lieutenant Commander Mike Blissett received orders from a controller aboard the frigate *Brilliant* to pursue a single Skyhawk that had just attacked another frigate, the *Ardent*, narrowly missing the ship with two 1,000-pound bombs. Diving to 1,500 feet in search of their prey, the Harriers spotted four other Skyhawks at lower altitude and more than three miles away. "As we passed over the top of them they saw us," Blissett recalled. "Their nice arrow formation broke up, and they began to jettison underwing tanks and bombs."

Desperate to escape, the Skyhawks broke hard right. The Sea Harriers followed closely and, from a range of about 400 yards, Blissett loosed a Sidewinder. "My first impression," he said later, "was that the missile was going to strike the ground as it fell away. Then suddenly it started to climb and rocketed toward the target." Just then, Blissett recalled, another Sidewinder "came streaming past my left shoulder—Neil had fired past me, which I found very disconcerting at the time." Instants later, both missiles struck their targets. One Skyhawk exploded in a huge fireball and, said Blissett,

During the entire six-week Falklands War, British ships in Falkland Sound came under Argentine air attack for a total of only seventy minutes or so, but among them were moments of intense danger and artful flying. In the top picture at right, an Argentine delta-winged Dagger flashes past the *Stromness* and the bow of the *Resource* as the two supply ships lie at anchor on the morning of May 24. Others flew even lower. Said one Navy gunner: "It was the first time I had to fire at an aircraft with the gun pointing down rather than up!" The center photograph shows an Argentine pilot's view of a bomb run against a British frigate as antiaircraft shells burst nearby. The North Sea ferry *Norland (bottom),* commandeered as a troopship, narrowly escapes disaster as bombs from a departing A-4 explode harmlessly on either side.

the other "came cartwheeling slowly past my aircraft about 100 yards away, looking like a slow-motion replay from a film."

By this time, attacks on the ships in Falkland Sound had begun to reveal the Argentines' battle plan and tactics. Perhaps fearing the loss of more Mirages to Sea Harriers or still feeling the need to defend mainland air bases, they would send no more fighter cover for their attack planes. Instead of saturating British defenses with large formations, the Argentines so far had sent their strikers in piecemeal, a few at a time. This puzzled the British, who also could not imagine why the strikes largely ignored British soldiers on the beaches and the vulnerable troop transports within the San Carlos anchorage, concentrating attacks almost entirely on warships abristle with weapons. Partly to avoid these defenses and partly because of having no air cover, the Daggers and A-4s rarely varied their style or axis of attack. As a British observer explained, they "would just fly by the contours of the land, come over the water, come in low, drop the payload, and afterburn their way out the other side."

Adjusting immediately to these patterns, the Sea Harrier pilots became rapidly more lethal. Following Blissett's and Thomas's victories, British aviators shot down six more enemy aircraft; two others fell to the fleet's missile and gun defenses. Such losses—20 percent of the fifty aircraft involved—could not be sustained for long even though the low-flying, hard-charging Argentines had inflicted grievous damage of their own: Twenty-four British seamen were dead; the *Ardent* was sinking; the *Antrim* and the *Argonaut* were out of action with unexploded bombs deep inside. The *Brilliant* and the *Broadsword* had suffered lesser damage.

Through it all, however, the British landings had continued. By nightfall, as the last pair of patrolling Sea Harriers returned to the *Hermes*, 3,000 troops had been landed on East Falkland. And there, steadily reinforced during the next several days, they would remain.

Despite their exertions, the Sea Harrier pilots who took their CAP stations the next day felt fit, fresh, and ready to fight—thanks to a strange quirk of circumstance. Throughout the war, the British set their clocks by Greenwich Mean Time, four hours ahead of time in the Falklands. "You could get up in the morning at eight o'clock body time, which was four o'clock local time," explained Flight Lieutenant Morgan. "So you wander along and have a good old shower, put a clean pair of knicks on and the lucky flying suit. Wander down, have a good breakfast. Walk out to the aircraft, get in, and launch just as the sun came over the horizon, feeling absolutely great." But, he added, the "poor old Spanish-speaking gentlemen had crawled out of their racks about three a.m. body time, and they were feeling like death by the time they hit the merge."

Yet weary or not, the Argentine airmen had plenty of fight in them, and on the early afternoon of May 23 four Skyhawks bowled into Falkland Sound and screamed straight at the frigate *Antelope*, which had come on station only four hours earlier as the replacement for her sister ship, the *Ardent*. One of the Skyhawks zipped in so low that it clipped the frigate's eighty-five-foot-high after mast about fifteen feet from the top. Amazingly, the A-4 suffered nothing worse than damage to a drop tank. A Skyhawk that followed it, however, fell to a missile from a nearby frigate.

Still, the strikers left two unexploded 1,000-pound bombs inside the *Antelope,* and that night, as demolition engineers attempted to defuse one of them, it exploded. The detonation killed only one man and injured three others, but it sparked a conflagration so fierce as to be unquenchable. While the crew abandoned ship, many of them lifted off by helicopter, fires spread to the missile magazines. They erupted, and early the next morning, the *Antelope* went down.

In the meantime, the British had sought to extend their early-warning capabilities by sending the *Broadsword* and the destroyer *Coventry* to positions north of West Falkland Island. There they would have a clear radar view of the route followed so far by most of the Argentine attack planes. Between the destroyer's Sea Darts, which had a range of well over twenty miles, and the frigate's Sea Wolves, the Royal Navy's most modern close-range missiles, the ships would have two chances at approaching enemy planes.

At about 10:15 a.m. on May 24, the redeployment paid off. Picking up a low, fast-flying flight on his radar, a *Broadsword* controller vectored a pair of Harriers to intercept the planes, which turned out to be Daggers. Within a few minutes, three of the four had been splashed by Sidewinders. These losses raised the number of Argentine planes shot down to twenty-four, 20 percent of their front-line aircraft—more than enough to persuade most air arms to call it quits. Yet the next day—May 25—would be the 171st anniversary of Argentina's War of Independence against Spain, and the fliers meant to have something to celebrate.

An explosion aboard HMS *Antelope* lights up sea and sky near San Carlos after fires ignited the frigate's missile magazine on the night of May 23. By morning, her hull broken, the ship had sunk, leaving only the bow and stern protruding above the water.

The symbolic significance of Argentina's national holiday was by no means lost on the British. Yet their top commanders rejected the suggestion that the *Broadsword* and the *Coventry* withdraw from their exposed position. Instead, they moved the carriers within eighty miles of the Falklands to provide additional time on CAP for the Harriers. Those decisions would be a formula for disaster.

As a first order of holiday business, the Argentines meant to rid themselves of the two radar picket ships. At 2:00 p.m., two pairs of Skyhawks came in over West Falkland, heading east as if to attack the beachheads, then veered north in a headlong dash toward the *Broadsword*. Radar operators aboard the *Coventry* saw them coming and vectored two Sea Harriers, flying CAP nearby, to intercept. Just as the jump jets dived to do so, however, the *Coventry* countermanded its order to attack. About to fire a Sea Dart missile, it wanted the Harriers out of the way. In the event, the Sea Dart missed, and the first pair of A-4s closed at 400 knots on the *Broadsword*, which attempted to fire a Sea Wolf missile.

"The aircraft were so low that some of our lookouts could see the wake of their jet streams on the water," said the *Broadsword's* skipper, Captain Bill Canning. Ordinarily, a Sea Wolf could acquire such targets, but this time the missiles refused to lock on—perhaps, Canning said, because "the two targets, wing tip to wing tip, confused the system." Moments later, the Skyhawks released their bombs at point-blank range.

Canning's ship had incredible luck. Three 1,000-pound bombs missed cleanly; a fourth skipped off the water, struck one side of the ship, passed upward through the deck, and dropped into the sea on the other side without exploding. The *Coventry* was not so fortunate. Three bombs from the second pair of Skyhawks smashed deep into the destroyer's bowels and exploded. Orbiting overhead, the pilot of a late-arriving Sea Harrier saw the vessel "listing badly, surrounded by lots of little orange dinghies and with helicopters all over the place. As we watched horrified, the huge ship rolled right over until she was upside down with only her propeller showing." Rescue efforts saved 283 British seamen, but 19 others perished.

At the very instant of the *Coventry's* destruction, a far greater threat to the British was developing 150 miles to the northeast, where the *Hermes* and the *Invincible* awaited the return of their aircraft. Aware that the task force had sailed to within 100 miles of Port Stanley, the Argentines had dispatched a pair of Super Etendards, armed with two of the three remaining AM-39 Exocets, from the Río Grande air base to seek out and destroy the British carriers.

Avoiding detection, the Etendards first flew 450 miles to the northeast. There, 240 miles north of the Falklands, they refueled from a KC-130 tanker. Then they headed east for several minutes before turning due south toward the carrier force. Approaching at 550 knots, the pilots popped up, switched on their radars—and saw images indicating two large ships and a smaller one dead ahead. At 3:38 p.m., only 22 miles from the nearest vessel, they launched the Exocets, broke away, and headed for home at high speed.

British countermeasures deflected one of the Exocets, and the other, instead of closing on one of the aircraft carriers, locked onto the frigate *Ambuscade*, northernmost ship in the British screen. Warned of the incoming missile by its own radar, the *Ambuscade* flashed a warning to the rest of the carrier force and then began firing chaff rockets. Confused by the reflective bits of aluminum foil, the Exocet flashed past the frigate, faltered, then acquired another target—the 15,000-ton supply ship *Atlantic Conveyor*.

Except for the carriers, the *Atlantic Conveyor* was the least expendable of the British ships. It not only carried thousands of tons of supplies that the troops ashore would soon need, but on its deck were lashed nine helicopters—three big Chinooks and six Wessex 5s—that British commanders considered vital to the support of their ground campaign.

From the bridge of the *Hermes*, an officer watched the developing calamity. "*Hermes* was in the center of the formation," he wrote later. "Ahead and slightly to the left was *Invincible*. *Atlantic Conveyor* was on our right, slightly ahead and about two miles away. All the warships were firing chaff rockets by this time; as ours went there would be a great 'whooosh' and against the darkening sky one could see the red flames from the receding rockets." But the *Atlantic Conveyor* had no chaff dispensers, and with unerring accuracy, the Exocet crashed into the big vessel's port side, exploding and blowing open a hole the size of a house. Twelve men were dead, and the cargo vessel sank three days later.

In retrospect, the convulsive Argentine effort of May 25 would be seen as a turning point in the Falklands air war. Despite its successes, the Argentine air arm had largely shot its bolt, and the

Harriers that took off from the *Hermes* and the *Invincible* next day had little to do but orbit their CAP sectors. Early that evening, British troops began to move out of the beachheads. By June 7, after a fortnight in which filthy weather offered more opposition than Argentina's ground or air forces, British forces converged on Port Stanley from the north and west as more troops landed on the southeast coast to open a third avenue of attack.

Argentina's pilots still had one punch left, and they delivered it there, in the southeast, on the clear, crisp afternoon of June 8. Early that morning, the landing ships *Sir Galahad* and *Sir Tristram* had put into the inlet at Fitzroy carrying two companies of the Welsh Guards, along with elements of other units. Various delays stretched the unloading through the morning and into the afternoon, well beyond the CAP window that was allotted to the landings. Thus, no Harriers were immediately at hand for the next

An Argentine soldier tries to bring a British-made Blowpipe missile to bear on a Harrier GR3 flying a particularly low level reconnaissance mission late in the war. Skimming past at high speed, the Royal Air Force pilot—who captured the action with his plane's camera—saw neither the missileer nor his two companions. "You concentrate on flying as low as you can," Flight Lieutenant Mark Hare later explained, "and missing the ground by as little as possible. I was concentrating on the staying alive bit!"

event. At 1:15 p.m., five Argentine A-4 Skyhawks roared across the Fitzroy inlet dropping bombs. Almost instantly, the *Sir Galahad* and the *Sir Tristram* exploded in flames that took fifty lives and injured fifty-seven men.

Too late, Harriers rushed to the scene. For most of the afternoon, the pilots could do little but circle overhead and gaze in anguish at the rescue efforts taking place below. Finally, toward dusk, Flight Lieutenant Dave Morgan and Lieutenant Dave Smith, flying the last mission of the day, spotted a Skyhawk far below, making a run at a small landing craft that was scurrying toward the shore. Morgan plunged in pursuit of the A-4—and flew straight into the war's wildest aerial melee.

While Morgan was on his way down, another Skyhawk appeared from nowhere, strafed the landing craft with cannon fire, and

dropped a bomb that struck the stern of the little vessel, killing six men. The sight of the attack on the defenseless boat made Morgan "more angry than I've ever been in my life. This is where it became very personal. I was not shooting down an aircraft. I was killing the guy in that aircraft. Definitely."

Then, however, a third Skyhawk flashed in front of Morgan and, off to the left, a fourth A-4 appeared. To have kept after the villain ahead of him would have left Morgan dangerously exposed to the fourth Skyhawk. So he hauled his Harrier into a high-G turn after this newest threat, pulled in behind, closed rapidly, and fired a Sidewinder straight up the tailpipe. "Very large explosion, huge fireball," said Morgan. "There was nothing bigger than a top hat that went into the water from the aircraft."

Now yet another Skyhawk angled across Morgan's nose. Again he fired a Sidewinder. Until now, all Harrier engagements had been straight tail chases that had not exploited the AIM-9L's all-aspect capabilities. This time, however, the enemy was passing in front of Morgan, offering only an oblique shot from abeam. "The missile came off the starboard rail and went straight across in front of my nose," Morgan related. "It's got a logic circuit in it that makes it aim for the shortest distance. It actually did this big turn in front of me and hit him right on the 90 degrees, just behind the cockpit. Everything aft just disintegrated as if you had a plastic model, put a shotgun to it, and pulled the trigger."

Two Skyhawks down. Two left, and they were scorching toward the west. Missiles gone, Morgan began firing his 30-mm cannon at

A Sea King helicopter winches up a crewman from the stricken landing ship *Sir Galahad* on the afternoon of June 8. Unable to see the horizon through the blinding smoke, helicopter pilots had to look around for other reference points. "The stern had the name *Sir Galahad* written on it in large letters," explained one pilot. "I used this as an artificial horizon."

The *Sir Galahad* continues to burn as survivors are hauled ashore on East Falkland. On June 26, the crippled 5,700-ton ship was towed out to sea and sunk as a grave for the sailors who did not escape.

one of them, but his gunsight malfunctioned, and the shots flew wild. All this time, Morgan recalled, his wingman, Dave Smith, had been trailing him, "seeing whoosh-bang, whoosh-bang, and not really knowing what was going on." Now, as Morgan climbed to break off, he cleared the way between Smith and the fleeing A-4. Smith fired a Sidewinder, and a third Skyhawk went down. The fourth vanished into the distance.

The attack at Fitzroy, the most grievous injury inflicted on British soldiers during the Falklands War, proved to be the dying thrust of Argentina's air arm as British troops, supported by Harriers from the sky and naval gunfire from the sea, inexorably tightened their choke hold on Port Stanley. By June 14, they could look down on the town from the north and west.

In the south, a small eminence called Sapper Hill remained as one of the last defensive positions still in Argentine possession. At 12:25 that afternoon, a pair of RAF GR3s arrived carrying laser-guided bombs, which the Harriers had started using only the day before. Seeking final permission to attack, they radioed an air controller on the ground. He had just received a frantic call from a Royal Marine commander on a nearby hill. "For Christ sake, hold it!" he cried. "The Argies are standing up on Sapper Hill and I think there's a white flag . . . Yes, there's a white flag . . . There's another white flag . . . It looks as if they're giving in. For Christ sake stop that attack!" The war for the Falklands was over. ★

Against a backdrop of rolling waves and a force 10 gale, a Sea Harrier armed with an AIM-9L Sidewinder sits lashed to the deck of the *Hermes* as the carrier sails home in the company of the frigate *Broadsword* and the carrier *Invincible.* During the war, this aircraft shot down two helicopters, raided Goose Green, and disabled an Argentine spy trawler. Long thought of as just a crowd pleaser at airshows, the Harrier had at last proved itself a potent and dangerous adversary.

An Epic Convening of Flattops

An F-14 Tomcat strikes out over the Red Sea from the *John F. Kennedy* on January 17, 1991, while another Tomcat, armed with Sidewinder, Sparrow, and Phoenix missiles, taxies aft. Planes from the *Kennedy* and three other carriers in the Red Sea and Persian Gulf attacked Iraq that day, the first of Operation Desert Storm.

The stars of Orion the Hunter hung high in the moonless sky, lending their pale light to the broad phosphorescent wakes of the *America*, the *Saratoga*, and the *John F. Kennedy* as the huge aircraft carriers, fifty miles apart, sailed with their escorts through the Red Sea. Together, the three groups of ships constituted a carrier battle force, an armada the likes of which had not been seen in combat since World War II. It was 1:00 a.m. on January 17, 1991, and Operation Desert Shield was about to become Operation Desert Storm.

On this night, the *America* had drawn the rotational duty of conducting combat air patrols to protect the forty ships of the three carrier battle groups from attack. At several points north of the Red Sea, toward Iraq, two-plane sections of F-14 Tomcat fighters orbited at 25,000 feet, and other Tomcats stood poised on five-minute deck alert. While the *America* stood guard, the massive strikes that would open the naval air war against Iraq would come from the *Saratoga* and the *Kennedy*.

Both carriers had already launched their first aircraft: the turboprop E-2C Hawkeyes that would serve as airborne warning and control (AWACS) platforms for the assault. The Hawkeyes would soon be orbiting slowly at 22,000 feet over Saudi Arabia, whence they could peer into Iraq with farseeing electronic eyes. And from the carriers also came a handful of KA-6 tankers, derivatives of the A-6E Intruder attack plane fitted for air-to-air refueling. The KA-6s set course for a point over Saudi Arabia about 100 miles from Iraq's border. There they would rendezvous with Air Force KC-135 tankers and help to refuel the planes of the carrier strike packages. All the while, an SH-3 Sea King helicopter known as an Angel to fliers had been hovering 300 feet above the water off each carrier's starboard side, ready to attempt a rescue if a launch went awry.

Now, as the hour arrived to launch the strike, the decks of the *Saratoga* and the *Kennedy* came alive with the glowing batons of plane directors motioning pilots toward catapults against a background of whining aircraft engines. With the Stars and Stripes snapping in the wind, the voice of the *Saratoga*'s captain rasped over the loudspeaker: "All right, men. This is the real thing. Let's go out and do it." A young pilot later remembered "chill bumps running up and down me. Seeing the American flag in the middle of the night and getting ready to go to war, it's a feeling you can't put into words."

After the Hawkeyes, first to queue up at the *Kennedy*'s catapults were eighteen vintage A-7E Corsair II light attack planes, lovingly known to their pilots as SLUFs (for "short little ugly fellows") and now the last of their kind in active carrier service. Aboard most of the other carriers in the gulf, the Corsairs had been replaced by F/A-18 Hornets, state-of-the-art supersonic aircraft that could perform as fighters or strikers—and by sundown two of the *Saratoga*'s twenty-two Hornets would convincingly demonstrate their lethal versatility. Behind the A-7s followed ten equally venerable A-6E Intruders, aircraft that first saw service in the early 1960s. Each A-6 could deliver up to 16,000 pounds of ordnance with pinpoint accuracy. "We fly an ugly airplane, a slow airplane, an old airplane," said one aviator, "but we get a lot of work done."

Next came four snub-nosed EA-6B Prowlers, electronic siblings of the A-6, each carrying sophisticated radar-jamming equipment and armed with HARMs (high-speed antiradiation missiles) that could track enemy radar transmissions to their source and pepper it with thousands of steel cubes. Last in line were the supersonic shepherds, four missile-armed F-14 Tomcats that would escort the strike forces deep into Iraq and protect them from enemy fighters.

On board the carriers, both the men and their machines were as ready as years of training and months of meticulous maintenance could make them. Each crew member, laden with forty pounds of flight gear, had strapped a small clipboard holding cards inscribed with mission details to his thigh, just above the knee. "The kneeboard cards," said one flier, "are your brain, stapled in the upper left-hand corner." To help conceal their identity should they be shot down, the aircrews stripped squadron and name patches from their flight suits, replacing them with glint tape—Velcro-backed strips that would reflect infrared searchlights beamed from rescue helicopters. "If they don't see that tape on someone," said an F-14 radar intercept officer, or RIO, "they shoot them."

On the *Kennedy,* as the first Corsair moved to one of the four steam catapults, a green-shirted hookup man crawled under the plane and connected the nose gear to the catapult shuttle protruding from a long slot in the flight deck. The catapult officer, wearing a yellow shirt and green helmet, waved his green wand back and forth, instructing the man at the controls to go to full power. As the throbbing aircraft strained against a holdback bar that kept it in check, the pilot moved his stick to the left, then the right, then forward and backward—"wiping out the cockpit," pilots called it—to check his flight controls. Then he turned on his navigation lights to show that he was ready. Seconds later, the plane was airborne, catapulted to flying speed of 150 knots in less than 300 feet.

One after another, the *Kennedy* hurled its warplanes aloft at a rate of nearly two per minute. Within twenty-two minutes all thirty-nine had blasted into the night, and after the last F-14 cleared the flight deck with a Vesuvian blast of its afterburners, half a score yellow shirts of the cat crew leaped into the air and slapped hands in a jet-age high-five.

By this point, it was 2:00 a.m. With the same flawless efficiency, all forty of the *Saratoga*'s strike aircraft had been launched as well. More was to come. About thirty minutes later and 1,000 miles to the east, another pair of strike packages began launching from the carriers *Ranger* and *Midway*, stationed in the Persian Gulf and soon to be joined by the *Theodore Roosevelt*. Nearly eighty strong, these planes constituted the second half of the U.S. Navy's massive one-two punch, the first of many such blows to be leveled at the forces of Iraqi strongman Saddam Hussein.

The Gulf War would last forty-three days. During that time, more than 500 planes from six U.S. carriers would fly more than 18,000 sorties, approximately one-sixth of the entire aerial effort against Iraq. Missions would take off around the clock, seven days a week—an average of about 425 per day. A modest percentage would be devoted to combat air patrol and other means of defending the battle group, the first essential task of carrier aviation, but the majority would take the war to the enemy, delivering more than 21 million pounds of ordnance onto the enemy's military machine and war-making infrastructure. And while the Navy had steeled itself to the loss of one or two planes per mission, the actual cost was a minuscule six aircraft and an equal number of aviators downed in combat,

with another six machines and two men victims of operational losses resulting from causes other than enemy action.

In a seaborne projection of air power never before accomplished, the U.S. Navy would wage two distinct campaigns against Iraq, each unfolding according to its own violent script. For much of the war, the three carriers in the Red Sea would contribute mightily to the assault against high-priority targets in western Iraq: Saddam Hussein's nuclear and chemical installations, his biggest and most critical airfields, and the launching areas for his Scud ballistic missiles. To do so, naval aviators would fly meticulously planned missions of exhausting length into the teeth of an air defense that made Vietnam seem tame by comparison. Aircraft from carriers cruising

Transfusion at Sea

After only a couple of weeks' combat, a carrier can expect to run out of fuel for its jets—a matter of little consequence, since by that time it would also have used up its bombs. To prevent carriers and the ships of their battle groups from having to frequently return to port for resupply, the Navy replenishes them as they steam along, keeping them at sea for up to nine months and more.

Three types of ships constitute the bulk of the underway-replenishment (UNREP) fleet: oilers bearing hundreds of thousands of barrels of aviation and diesel fuel, ammunition ships loaded with ordnance, combat stores ships carrying everything from ice cream to toilet paper. A fourth type, the fast combat support ship, combines all three roles, reducing the time warships must spend consorting with their tenders.

In anticipation that enemy action could separate a fleet from its supply lifeline for many a week or longer, replenishment occurs often. Every two or three days during the Gulf War, for example, each ship of the

carrier battle groups topped off fuel tanks that remained up to 90 percent full. At the same time, the vessels took on other stores.

During replenishment, twin-rotor CH-46 Sea Knight helicopters based on the support ships transfer much that can be packed in crates or lashed to pallets. Refueling, however, demands the use of high-pressure hoses, passed across from an oiler. The two ships first match speed and heading, then position themselves a couple of hundred feet apart. Using modified rifles, crew members fire lightweight lines across the gap. Other lines—one spliced with a flag every twenty feet to help gauge separation between ships—are pulled across. They are followed by cables to support the hoses. Made fast to the recipient vessel, the cables are held at 8,000 pounds tension by hydraulic machinery aboard the UNREP ship that can compensate for variations in the space between the vessels up to fifty feet. Then the hoses are trollied across the cables and plugged into receptacles *(overleaf)*.

The fast combat support ship *Sacramento* simultaneously replenishes a carrier and an Aegis cruiser during Desert Storm. The 53,000-ton ship can do its job in any weather, day or night.

the Persian Gulf, meanwhile, would fly shorter, more frequent missions concentrated on Saddam's tanks, artillery, and infantry dug into the sands of eastern Iraq and Kuwait.

Carriers operating from the Red Sea and the Persian Gulf—plus Air Force planes based ashore in Saudi Arabia—allowed the air war to proceed on three axes simultaneously. "Saddam didn't know where the threat would be coming from," a Navy official explained later. "He had to worry about the seas to his southwest and the southeast, not just Saudi Arabia in the south."

Another aspect distinguished air operations in the gulf conflict from those in earlier wars. In Vietnam, for example, the Navy and the Air Force flew against separate geographical regions. This seg-

A wheeled trolley carries two refueling hoses along a cable strung between a fleet oiler and an aircraft carrier. The metal proboscis at the end of each hose snaps into a fitting that leads to fuel tanks aboard the vessel receiving the fuel.

Shackled to the ship by safety lines, riggers stand by as fuel flows through a hose at the rate of 3,000 gallons per minute.

regation allowed the two services to operate autonomously. No such arrangement obtained in the gulf, a circumstance that required unprecedented coordination. Renowned for charting its own course, "the Navy had never wanted to be part of a centrally directed campaign," explained Captain Steven Ramsdell, director of naval aviation history at the time. "The ethic of independence, and being free to do our own thing, is powerful, and we're very leery of anything that appears to threaten that." During Desert Storm, however, the admirals willingly took orders in aviation matters from an Air Force general who, in turn, was responsible to an Army commander in chief. "It worked," Ramsdell said later. "It worked a lot better than anyone in the Navy ever would have guessed."

en with two such conduits,
upplying an aircraft carrier
h jet fuel can take as long as
r hours or more.

Rough seas offer little hin-
drance to replenishment opera-··
tions. Such conditions, however, tax the skills and stamina of
the helmsman and the officer on
the bridge charged with main-
taining the appropriate distance
between ships.

For the carriers, the synchronization process began before dawn, forty-eight hours before the bombs were to fall, at the carrier-battle-force level. Battle Force Zulu, headquartered aboard the *Midway*, comprised all the carriers in the gulf; the flagship for Battle Force Yankee in the Red Sea was the *Kennedy*.

Aboard each ship, and headed by the battle-force commander, was a planning staff called the strike cell, which monitored the combat status of all the ships and aircraft in its battle force hour by hour, drew up a list of assignments, and passed the recommendations to Joint Forces Air Component Command (JFACC) in Riyadh, Saudi Arabia—and there began the staggering task of fitting them into an enormous document called the air tasking order. The ATO, as it was called, dictated the daily activity of each of the more than 2,000 sea- and land-based aircraft arrayed against Saddam by a UN-sponsored coalition of powers intent on ejecting Iraq from Kuwait.

Starting at 9:00 a.m., liaison officers from the gulf and Red Sea carrier battle forces, working with coordinators from the U.S. Air Force and coalition air forces, pored over the latest intelligence reports. They studied banks of twenty-inch computer monitors that displayed potential targets as blue triangles and targets that had been hit in yellow. Destroyed targets had red markers. By the same time the following morning, the next day's ATO, some 600 pages long, was usually complete. Riyadh transmitted the entire tasking order to Air Force squadrons by high-speed encrypted teletype. This communications system, however, had been developed especially for Air Force operations in Europe and had not been installed on aircraft carriers. So great would have been the time needed for the carriers to receive the ATO electronically by way of their slower system that each battle force detailed an S-3 Viking antisubmarine aircraft to fly the next day's ATO to the ships.

Targets for the war's opening three days, however, had been chosen during the preceding months. Planes from Battle Force Yankee in the Red Sea would first hit, among other targets, Hussein's chemical warfare plants at Samarra, northwest of Baghdad; the airfield at Al Taqqadum, west of the city; then follow up with strikes at the airfields known as H2 and H3 in the western Iraqi desert near Jordan. Battle Force Zulu, in the central Persian Gulf, would launch two equally destructive strikes, one after the other, at the major naval base at Umm Qasr, tucked in behind a mosaic of islands just north of Kuwait. For all that, Navy planners had pointed a majority of the aircraft at enemy air defenses in the target areas.

Onslaught from the Red Sea

Strike packages from the *Saratoga* and the *Kennedy* had flown more than 500 miles from the Red Sea as they neared the Iraqi border; forming into flights after takeoff and aerial refuelings had made the trip a two-hour journey. The sixty strikers and shepherds had already topped off their tanks as many as four times, snuggling up to the big Air Force KC-135s and their own Navy KA-6s, whose presence doubled the speed of the refueling operation. Each KA-6 took position off the starboard wing of a KC-135, and the strike aircraft could thus refuel in pairs. When a Navy tanker ran low, it would take on more fuel from the big Air Force craft, then resume its position. After a refueling 100 miles south of the Iraqi border, the Air Force tankers advanced no farther than 100 miles south of Iraq, but the KA-6s continued with the strike force. Just short of the enemy border, they topped off the F-14s, providing them with as much fuel as possible for tangling with Iraqi fighters.

Then, just before streaking into Iraq, the planes "went midnight." Aircrews shut down everything that could announce their presence, from running lights to radar transponders that would be used on returning from the mission to identify the aircraft as friendly to coalition air defenses. As the aircraft crossed the border, the *Kennedy* broadcast a radio message addressed to fighters flying combat air patrol in defense of the carriers: "Warning red. Weapons tight." "Red" meant that hostilities had begun, and "tight" imposed rules of engagement that restricted the fliers from firing without positive identification of an enemy, either by eye or from one of the airborne warning and control aircraft on station for the events. The war was on.

For men embroiled in the turmoil of combat—and especially for neophytes—memory plays curious tricks, account-

At the start of Desert Storm, aircraft carriers in the Red Sea concentrated on strategic targets in central and western Iraq, while flattops in the Persian Gulf hit objectives in eastern Iraq and Kuwait (inset). By mid-February, with most targets on the allies' strategic list destroyed and a ground war imminent, all six carriers had Iraqi troops and tanks added to their target lists.

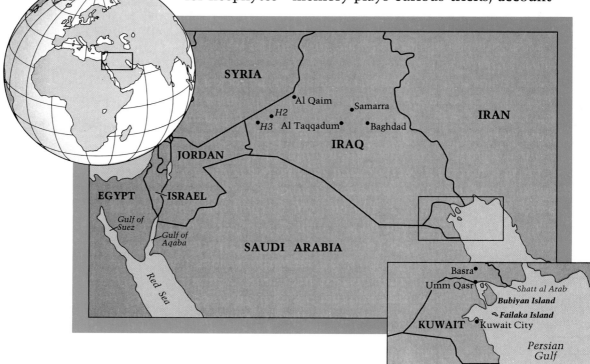

ing for sketchy recollections of specific details about that January night over Iraq. Some fliers had difficulty remembering what targets they attacked. Nonetheless, airmen from the *Saratoga* and the *Kennedy* would retain vivid impressions of sudden, pyrotechnic violence.

As the strikes approached their targets, Iraq's deeply layered antiaircraft artillery opened up. To an untried Tomcat pilot from the *Saratoga*, the first sight of antiaircraft artillery (AAA) fire at night was an awesome experience. "We would watch it and it would actually glow," he recalled. "It was like a living thing. It would get bigger. It would get smaller. It would move left. It would move right. It was an incredible thing to see a whole country dark, blacked out, except for these huge pockets of what looked like a living mass of light." To the F-14s coming in above 20,000 feet, the AAA offered more of a light show than a threat. Surface-to-air-missile batteries guarding the targets posed a greater peril, and as the carrier aircraft drew closer, SAM fire-control radar set off the screech of warning alarms in the aircrews' headsets. Time for the Prowlers to go to work.

Of all the aircraft employed by the Navy in Desert Storm, the electronic countermeasure Prowler came as close as any to being indispensable. For every carrier bombing mission, and for many USAF and coalition strikes as well, the EA-6s were essential. If Prowlers were unavailable, the attack planes stayed home.

Its quarter-of-a-million-dollar canopy coated with a transparent film of gold to protect occupants of the cockpit from the plane's own emissions—they would otherwise turn the cockpit into a microwave oven—the EA-6 carried as many as three jamming pods beneath its fuselage and wings, each one of which could not only jam radars but also knock out most communications for dozens of miles in every direction.

Now, at a range of about thirty miles, the Prowlers unleashed an

Late in the afternoon of January 16, just hours before the opening of the air war on Iraq, a brown-shirted plane captain on the *John F. Kennedy* climbs over a huffer, a combination jet-engine starter and tow truck. It sits in front of an EA-6B Prowler electronic-warfare aircraft (recognizable by its double canopies) and is flanked by laser-guided bombs, some perhaps destined for the last plane in the row of three, an A-6 Intruder.

electronic storm that overwhelmed Iraqi radar. Many enemy radar operators wisely switched off their sets; others turned up the power, trying to overcome the jamming, escaping the fate of those that did not: mach 3, radar-homing HARM missiles, hundreds of which were fired during the first two days of Desert Storm. To keep radars transmitting so that HARMs could find them, A-6 Intruders, A-7 Corsairs, and S-3 Vikings launched sleek gliders called TALDs, for tactical air-launched decoys. Descending swiftly toward Iraqi defenses, they mimicked the radar signatures of strike aircraft, attracting the attention of radars at SAM sites. Prowlers followed to launch HARMs at any transmitter that took the bait.

With Iraqi air defenses in disarray, four-plane divisions of F-14s flashed across the target area to sweep for interceptors. Following two and a half minutes behind came the strikers—the sturdy Intruders, the versatile Hornets, and the faithful old Corsairs.

For the aircrews of them all, the moment had arrived when the years of arduous training would be turned to deadly purpose. "What is going through my mind," one pilot said later of his first headlong rush into combat, "is 'Please, God, don't let me screw this up. Just let me do it right.'"

As the fighter-bombers attacked, more TALDs were launched from a different direction to confuse whatever radar remained. Heavy concentrations of AAA erupted from the ground but lacked the range to touch the Navy planes and were inaccurate to boot. Here and there, Iraqi SAM sites launched their missiles, the rocket exhausts reminding one pilot of the glowing ashes from a campfire climbing into the night. Hurled blindly, without radar guidance, none of the missiles connected. Orbiting over Saudi Arabia, the big Air Force AWACS aircraft with their all-seeing radar and the Navy's E-2C mini-AWACS reported few enemy planes aloft.

On a night mission, after acquiring the target by radar, an A-6 bombardier-navigator (B/N) typically matches up the view through the plane's forward-looking infrared (FLIR) system with the radar image, then places the FLIR cross hairs where the bombs are to strike. Locking this aiming point into the on-board bombing computer, the B/N initiates tracking, in which the system follows the progress of the aircraft toward the optimum release point. Informed by the B/N that the system is tracking, the pilot pulls the commit trigger on the control stick, authorizing the computer to drop the ordnance when the aircraft is in position. To fly it there, the pilot follows steering instructions from the computer. At the appropriate instant for a direct hit, the computer pickles off the bombs.

Feeling the lurch of bombs detaching from the wings, the planes turned southward, jinking violently out of Iraq toward a refueling rendezvous over Saudi Arabia. En route, each plane checked in with an E-2C Hawkeye monitoring the strike—and only then did the men learn that one of *Saratoga*'s F/A-18s was missing. Nobody had seen it go down, and for a while, the fliers hoped against hope that the pilot, running short of fuel, had merely landed at a Saudi airfield or, at worst, suffered battle damage and parachuted to safety. "I hope he's out in the desert right now," said one, "picking sand fleas out of his shorts." It was not to be: The Navy would eventually list thirty-three-year-old Lieutenant Commander Michael Speicher as killed in action—the first American airman to die in combat during Desert Storm.

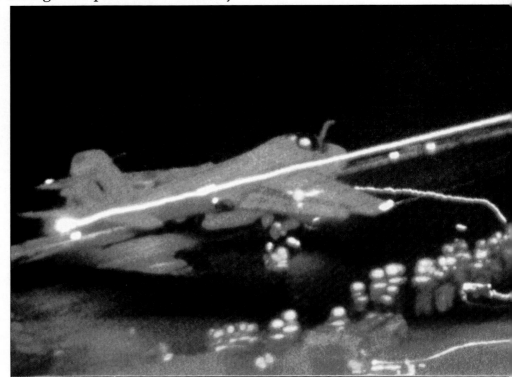

At 5:00 a.m., well before first light, the vanguard of the returning planes entered the landing pattern at the carriers. Nothing focuses a Navy pilot's attention like a night landing at sea, where darkness makes an already difficult feat far more demanding. Yet on

The *Saratoga's* flight deck offers an infernal light show in this time exposure of an A-6 Intruder preparing to take its place in a strike package headed for Iraq in early February 1991. A night catapult shot is "scary," said one pilot. "You have no control. You're along for the ride." In seconds, the plane jolts from the glow of the deck lights into a profound blackness. "On a dark night," continued the aviator, "it's like someone threw you in a closet and slammed the door."

this night, hooking an arrester cable seemed "almost anticlimactic because of all the stuff you'd never seen before," said one pilot. "I'd never seen bombs going off at night. I'd never seen a missile fired at night. So coming back to the carrier was difficult—but familiar." For this aviator—and all but a handful of the others as well—the missions of January 17 were a baptism. On the *Ranger*, only the air group commander, a Tomcat driver of forty-five, had seen combat—in Vietnam. After shutting down their engines, many of the fliers just sat in their planes for a moment, breathing deeply and letting the tension of the past five hours start to drain away.

Within three hours, maintenance crews and armorers had the planes ready for the first daytime strike missions against H2 and H3—heavily defended airfield complexes located in western Iraq near the Jordanian border. For the next forty-two days, at times working six days on and two days off, pilots flew one of these intensely demanding missions every day. Even with additional crews to fly the daylight strike packages, aircrews would be getting by on as little as four hours of sleep in every twenty-four.

Once again, Tomcats or Hornets in the lead and Prowlers just behind, the Intruders and Corsairs swept down to wreak their devastation. With daylight, more Iraqi aircraft were aloft—and finding themselves in the baleful presence of the Tomcats. Armed with Phoenix, Sparrow, and Sidewinder missiles and equipped with a powerful radar, the Tomcat is deadly out to ninety miles, and the Iraqis knew as much. Every time a Tomcat pointed its nose toward a contact, the bogeys turned tail and fled. "Our radar is so powerful that it would totally wipe out their warning gear," said a *Kennedy* F-14 RIO, who sat in the backseat of the plane. "They'd know an F-14 was stalking them. But our radar was just saturating their ears, so they didn't really know where we were. All they could do was run until their gear told them an F-14 wasn't there anymore."

Within minutes, the *Saratoga* and *Kennedy* fighters had cleared the skies ahead. First across the border, the *Kennedy*'s Tomcats alone had chased away three or four flights of Iraqi interceptors, no more than eight planes. All escaped save two—a pair of MiG-21 Fishbeds that blundered into the path of four *Saratoga* F/A-18 Hornets beginning a bombing run on H2.

Standard procedure for the dual-role F/A-18 is to enter enemy air space in its fighter mode, prepared to do battle with its air-to-air missiles and 20-mm cannon. Nearing their target, however, these Hornets had switched their weapons systems to ground-attack mode, blinding them to aerial threats and giving no indication of their presence to the Iraqi planes' on-board warning gear. Furthermore the MiGs, equipped with only the most rudimentary radar, did not detect the Hornets. However, an E-2C Hawkeye, orbiting over Saudi Arabia, took in the scene and flashed a terse alert to the Hornets. "Bandits on your nose. Fifteen nautical miles."

In the Hornet cockpits, the pilots had been concentrating on the "basics," as one of them, Lieutenant Commander Mark Fox, put it. "Keep sight. Keep quiet, fly good wing, find the target, and bomb it." But self-preservation came first, and now each pilot pressed a button that returned the Hornets to air-combat mode. On flashed the air-to-air radar. Lock on. Fox selected a heat-seeking Sidewinder, heard the angry growl signifying that the weapon's infrared seeker had found the target pointed out by the plane's radar, and squeezed the red trigger on his control stick. Then, seeing the Sidewinder appear to go astray, he launched a radar-guided Sparrow. Both missiles hit home, and the MiG fell. "As the flaming Fishbed passed below me," Fox recalled, "I rocked up on my left wing to watch him go by. The rear half of the tan MiG-21 was enveloped in flames."

Almost simultaneously, Lieutenant Nick Mongillo in another Hornet picked up on the second Fishbed, less than a mile away and closing rapidly. "I was sure he was a bad guy," said Mongillo, "so I initiated a Sparrow and watched it guide to a direct hit a half-mile away." And as the MiGs exploded on the ground, there came Mongillo's excited cries on the radio: "Splash One! . . . Splash Two!"

Circumstances would make these victories—and one over a hapless Iraqi helicopter—the Navy's only air-to-air kills of the Gulf War. Though supremely satisfying, however, they were mere asides to the primary mission that day of bombing hangars and headquarters buildings at H2. With another simple press of the button, the pilots returned to the air-to-ground mode, rolled into their dives, and released four 2,000-pound Mark 84 unguided bombs apiece smack on target.

After Speicher's F/A-18, no more U.S. planes were downed on January 17, but in the predawn hours of the 18th—on another mission against H2—two *Saratoga* Intruders were lost. One badly damaged plane made an emergency landing; the crew escaped injury, but the A-6 had to be scrapped. The other, manned by Lieutenants Robert Wetzel and Jeffrey Zaun, took a hit from a SAM. Both fliers ejected safely over Iraq and were taken prisoner.

When struck, Zaun had been flying a low-level attack in an effort to surprise the enemy and to evade the worst of Iraqi air defenses. Low altitude, although it increased the danger from AAA fire, reduced the effectiveness of SAMs and fighter interception. It quickly became evident, however, that the missiles could be neutralized through electronic warfare and that the Iraqi Air Force was loath to fight. Upon realizing that massed Iraqi guns, which could raise curtains of steel up to 12,000 feet even without radar, had become the greatest threat, Battle Force Yankee ordered all attack planes to make their approaches at no less than 20,000 feet, drop their ordnance above 16,000 feet, and pull out of their dives at a height greater than two miles above the ground.

Little is certain in warfare, and such tactics could not guarantee against casualties. In the early-morning darkness of January 21, while cruising at 26,000 feet over central Iraq, one of the *Saratoga*'s newest F-14-pluses—a model with more powerful engines than the original—fell to an SA-2. A pilot must see this missile in order to evade it, but that morning an overcast hid the rocket exhaust from view until it was too late.

Four *Saratoga* planes had gone down in the war's first five days. The grim numbers aroused unspoken fears that the gallant *Saratoga* had somehow become a jinxed ship. Neither the *Kennedy*'s nor the *America*'s air wing had suffered so much as a bullet hole. But the proud old flattop, commissioned in 1956, would not lose another plane during the war. Indeed, spirits rose at the announcement that an Air Force special-operations helicopter had rescued the downed Tomcat driver. (His RIO also survived, but as a prisoner.)

During the Gulf War, many new weapons saw combat for the first time. Among them was a Navy missile, still being evaluated after fewer than a dozen tests, called the standoff land-attack missile (SLAM), several of which were rushed to the war zone. Although many details of their use remain classified, it is known that on the early morning of January 21, an A-6 catapulted off the *Kennedy*'s flight deck carrying two SLAMs under its wings. A weapon of decidedly mixed pedigree *(pages 130-131)*, the SLAM could score a

Lieutenant Devon Jones, a Tomcat pilot from the *Sarat[oga]* runs toward a U.S. Special O[p]erations airman sent to fetch him from the Iraqi desert 16[0] miles north of the Saudi Ara[bian] border. Jones had ejected fro[m] his F-14 before dawn on Janu ary 21, after a surface-to-air [mis]sile shredded the plane's rud[der.] Burying his parachute, the p[ilot] spent the morning in a shall[ow] trench that he dug for conce[al]ment. At noon, he answered

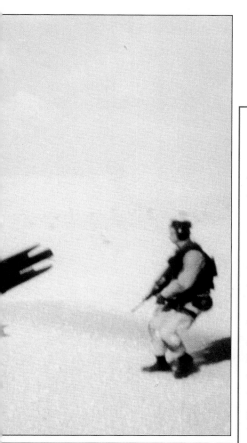

...l from an A-10 Warthog pilot
... his survival radio. Dis-
...tched to find him, the A-10
...lot relayed the location to an
...-53 Special Operations heli-
...pter already en route from
...udi Arabia, then, just as the
...opper was about to touch
...wn two hours later, shot up
... Iraqi truck that he saw racing
...ward the anxious flier. Said
...nes: "I had never seen such a
...autiful sight as that big,
...own, American H-53."

ringer every time with a 500-pound warhead launched from a point safely beyond the reach of enemy defenses—if it worked.

The *Kennedy*'s SLAM-armed Intruder headed toward an oft-visited target, a uranium-processing complex at Al Qaim, in the western desert. Flanked by four SA-3 and two SA-2 sites along with countless triple-A batteries, this nuclear facility boasted perhaps the heaviest defenses of any target in Iraq outside of Baghdad. Flying at 15,000 feet and still more than fifty miles away from the target, the A-6 unleashed the first of its SLAMs. As the missile sped on its way, it came under the control of a standoff A-7 Corsair *(pages 130-131).* Watching a video screen linked to the infrared imager in the nose of the missile, the Corsair pilot locked the weapon onto a door at one end of a long building used for refining uranium for bombs, then saw the picture turn to snow as the SLAM smashed through the portal. Seconds later, another SLAM, fired by the Intruder and controlled by the Corsair, hurtled through the now-gaping doorway and exploded inside the reinforced concrete structure. "My eyes were as big as saucers," said the A-7 driver, "watching the second missile go into the first hole."

The Navy's aviators attacked day and night through the first week. But then the weather turned foul, forcing the cancellation of some operations and creating new hazards for the fliers.

Even in fair weather, aerial refueling was a tricky process. "We're talking about thirty or thirty-five planes meeting these four tankers 500 feet apart," explained an A-6 pilot from the *America*, which had rotated off its defensive CAP assignment and joined the onslaught against Iraq. Noted an aviator from the *Kennedy:* "I had airplanes cut us off in the pattern, turn right inside us because they didn't see us. And that's in good weather."

Furthermore, Air Force KC-135 and KC-10 pilots, following the advice in their manuals for tanking Navy aircraft, initially flew at about 435 knots—too fast for a fighter or bomber pilot to keep the aircraft's refueling probe in the basket *(pages 132-133)* while bucking the wake of a tanker. This delicate task requires constant work with stick and throttle. If the speed is too high, even by as little as 30 knots in the thin air above 20,000 feet where most refueling takes place, subtlety with the stick becomes all but impossible. The slightest correction brings too great a response. In addition, heavily

An A-6 Intruder launches a SLAM during free-flight testing before Operation Desert Storm.

AIRCRAFT CARRIER

A Precision Arrow for the Navy's Quiver

As humans sometimes are, machines can become confused by the fog of war. For example, a radar-guided missile launched at a target in a cluttered setting—a warship among merchantmen at anchor in a crowded port, or a command center sited among innocuous buildings—is more likely to miss than one sent toward an isolated target: Confronted with multiple radar returns, the missile might home on the wrong one. Even if the weapon succeeds in locking onto the right one, it will always fly toward the center of the echo, where protective armor or reinforced concrete may well be thickest.

Navy pilots sent to cripple the heavily defended nuclear facility at Al Qaim during Desert Storm faced all these problems; they overcame them with the standoff land-attack missile, or SLAM. This low-cost weapon, which was still undergoing operational evaluation when it was rushed into combat, had been built using a Harpoon antiship missile as a foundation. A satellite-aided navigation system, accurate to within twenty yards, guides the missile to the vicinity of the target. There, instead of radar homing, the SLAM uses the infrared seeker of a Maverick antitank missile and the video transmitter of a Walleye glide bomb.

Near the end of the flight, the transmitter sends a video image of the objective to an airborne controller, who steers the SLAM toward impact using a small control stick. The controller may be the pilot who launched the missile or, as shown at right, a second aviator in a different aircraft. Flying in relative safety some eighty miles behind the missile, the controller verifies that the view from the SLAM's infrared seeker shows the target, then fine-tunes the path of the missile so that its 500-pound warhead hammers the target at its softest point.

A-7 CONTROL AIRCRAFT

A-6 LAUNCH AIRCRAFT

Nearly 100 miles from the target, an A-6 Intruder launches a SLAM on its ground-hugging flight, then heads for its ship. The missile, meanwhile, using data from Global Positioning System satellites to stay on course and a radar altimeter to avoid hills and other obstacles, heads for target coordinates programmed into the guidance system earlier. As the missile approaches the preset coordinates, its infrared seeker and video transmitter switch on, and the SLAM beams a picture of the target to the pilot of the control aircraft, an A-7 Corsair. Having put his plane on autopilot, he can focus his attention on steering the missile to the optimum point of impact.

laden A-6s and A-7s had insufficient thrust in reserve to inch forward slightly when necessary to maintain contact with the basket. "I don't think any of us had ever tanked off a '135 or KC-10 with ordnance, which is much more difficult," said one A-6 flier. "Usually we have plenty of power, and there we were strapped for power." At times, even F-14s and F/A-18s had to tap their afterburners to keep up with the airborne gas stations, and with the burners lit, the fighters consumed fuel faster than it flowed through the hose. But tanker pilots soon learned to fly at about 400 knots, greatly facilitating refueling operations.

As miserable weather enveloped the region, carrier pilots found themselves "flying around fishing for tankers in solid goo," as the RIO of one F-14 put it. "I looked on the radar, and there were tankers everywhere—six different tankers with little airplanes joining and leaving them. In good weather, you can see the guy ten miles away, sometimes twenty. So there we are, we'd already gotten down to two miles, and we just don't see him. We get down to a mile and I'm calling off points of a mile, saying, 'He's point nine miles ahead. We've got ten knots overtake.' Then, point eight, point seven, point six. We got all the way down to point one. We're within 600 feet and we still don't see him. And all of a sudden he kind of just loomed out of the mist—a big gray mass, right in front of us. My skipper was kissing my feet after that, because without our radar we would have been lost."

As unnerving as such encounters could be, the more significant danger of midair collision arises between pilots who are unaware of each other's presence. With thousands of planes maneuvering in a relatively small patch of sky, such encounters were a constant worry. Yet the command and control aloft exerted by the Navy's Hawkeyes and the Air Force AWACS proved so exact that not one such mishap occurred during the entire forty-three days of Desert Storm. Of equal concern was the ever-present possibility of a "blue-on-blue" situation, with friendlies firing on friendlies. At certain angles, the Panavia Tornado flown by the Royal Air Force and the Saudi Arabian Air Force bore an unsettling resemblance to Iraq's Soviet-made MiG-23 Flogger.

A Navy A-6 Intruder, carrying a load of fuel instead of bombs, and an Air Force KC-135 Strato-tanker top off a pair of EA-6B Prowlers over Saudi Arabia, while a third Prowler *(fore-ground)* stands by. During the war, Navy fliers came to call the smaller plane the Jesus tanker because it could fly north from its orbit over Saudi Arabia to meet a pilot running low on fuel who might otherwise have to eject over enemy territory.

The pace of operations was exhausting, as deck hands matched aircrews hour for grueling hour. Ordinarily, at sea a sailor will work an eighty-one-hour week. But in combat, the men sometimes labored eighteen to twenty hours a day, grabbing coffee and cold sandwiches—no time for hot meals—and catching forty winks where they could. Red-shirted ordnancemen sweated to fit bombs with fuzes and tail fins and load them onto elevators headed for the flight deck. No one lost an opportunity to decorate the casings with messages for Saddam Hussein, and they took pleasure in occasional visits from the admiral or captain or air group commander to tell them what mission their bombs were slated for.

Topside, everyone pitched in to get the planes serviced and rearmed, and fifty-minute turnarounds became routine. Cooks and typists stood shoulder to shoulder with the ordnancemen—ordies—everybody heaving and grunting to get the bombs and missiles onto the planes. Each flattop depleted its stock of ordnance at the rate of 500 to 1,000 bombs and missiles daily, so rapidly that replenishment ships came alongside virtually every day. More than once, a carrier launching aircraft loaded with the last of the ordnance could be seen simultaneously restocking the magazines from a supply ship steaming a few dozen yards off the starboard side. Restocking continued even at night, when helicopters hovered low over the decks to deliver weapons by sling.

The deck sometimes offered uncertain footing. A nonskid compound covers the steel flight deck of a carrier to improve traction. But hundreds of takeoffs and landings a day and frequent repositioning of planes eventually polished the flight deck to bare metal. Decks of the *Kennedy* and the *Saratoga,* in poor condition when the ships set sail for the Mideast, deteriorated rapidly. Accumulating oil and grease reminded one aviator of "a dirty frying pan" and created a slippery hazard to man and machine. So the crew scrubbed the decks when the planes were aloft, one-third at a time, day and night. Sprayers with tanks of detergent and water walked ahead, followed by ranks of men wielding stiff-bristled push brooms.

Despite this effort, footing could become so treacherous that plane handlers had to use two tractors—one forward to pull and one aft as a steadying counterweight—to move planes about the deck. Aircraft taxiing under their own power had no such security. On one occasion, one of the *Saratoga*'s F-14s started sliding toward the edge of the slanting deck as the pilot approached a catapult. He applied the brakes and tried to steer away from danger, but the $40 million Tomcat was on its way over the side. The plane captain, who had just finished checking the F-14 prior to launch and had removed the tie-down chains, quickly sized up the situation. In a flash, he dived under the engine inlets and jammed his chains between the deck and the slipping tires, bringing the plane to a halt. The pilot reported that he and his backseater were seconds from ejecting. "All he could see was water," said the plane captain later.

Remarkably, not a single plane was lost or even seriously damaged by the slippery deck conditions. Nor did they prevent the planes from thundering aloft with terrible regularity. One prime target was the Scud ballistic missiles Hussein was using as terror weapons against Israel, hoping to draw the Israelis into the war and thus shatter the Arab coalition aligned against him. Day and night, flights of A-6 Intruders, F/A-18 Hornets, and A-7 Corsairs patrolled seventy-mile-square sectors of southwestern Iraq helping the Air Force exterminate the elusively mobile Scud launchers.

To keep score against the Scuds and against the airfields, industrial plants, communications centers, and other strategic installations that continued to suffer the bulk of the Navy sorties, accurate bomb-damage assessment was desperately needed. So that Navy carriers would have the ability to perform their own reconnaissance, engineers had designed TARPS (tactical air reconnaissance pod system) for the supersonic F-14 Tomcat. Slung beneath the centerline of the fighter, the pod contained a versatile suite of photographic and infrared sensors *(pages 140-141)*.

Taking pictures might not be as satisfying as splashing MiGs, but a recon mission like one that occurred on February 12 could capture any flier's ardent attention. By then, the uranium-processing complex at Al Qaim—known aboard the *Kennedy* as Big Al's Place—had been hammered by everything from SLAMS to laser-guided bombs and Mark 20 Rockeye cluster munitions. It had even been carpet-bombed by Air Force B-52s. Despite the pounding, the Iraqis thought the site worthy of ferocious defense. Wrecked SAM and AAA equipment, which had already claimed an Air Force F-15E ground-attack plane, had been replaced, and the Iraqi defenses continued to operate at full force.

And so, on this morning, an F-14 with Lieutenant James Kuhn as pilot, Lieutenant Commander David Parsons as RIO, and a TARPS pod under the belly catapulted from the *Kennedy*'s flight deck,

bound for Al Qaim. Because of the danger to a photorecon plane penetrating Big Al's formidable SAM envelope, Kuhn and Parsons flew with a quintet of accompanists: an EA-6 Prowler equipped with jammers, an A-7 Corsair carrying three HARMs, a pair of TARPS-equipped Tomcats to take duplicate pictures and fend off any Iraqi fighters that might challenge them, and a third F-14 to protect the Prowler and the Corsair from enemy planes.

Kuhn and Parsons, who usually bantered amiably over the jet's intercom, were subdued on this risky mission. As the formation neared Al Qaim, recalled Kuhn, "we were instantly lit up by the SAMs and guns. But that was okay because they got HARMs in their faces for bothering us." In fact, the Iraqis got three HARMs fired one after the other, and then Kuhn and Parsons started their run, kicking in afterburners and tobogganing down from 30,000 feet to 20,000 feet for added speed and clearer pictures. Weighed down with fuel and held back by the drag of the air-to-air missiles and the recon pod it carried, the Tomcat could make only mach 1.2, about 60 percent of its "clean" speed. The ground seemed to creep past, and Parsons called out over the intercom to Kuhn: "Faster!" The pilot yelled back: "I'm going as fast as I can!"

One of the Tomcat escorts flew beside them, and both planes were jinking back and forth as they zigzagged toward the target. Four pairs of eyes scanned the ground intently for the telltale dust cloud of a SAM launch. "You have to keep looking for the SAMs because if you see the launch you can probably evade the missile," said Parsons. Down they dived, and after an eternity, they were in camera range. Kuhn said to himself: "Check cameras running. Settle down for just a moment. Make it easier on the cameras. Then back with a little duck to the right, and slice to the left."

Jinking wildly, the Tomcats hauled off the target and headed home. There was a final moment of high anxiety when Kuhn, looking back, hollered, "SAM! Eight o'clock!" But Parsons recognized the smoke as the dirty gray puff of a HARM exploding, not the brown cloud of a SAM launch, and no missile rose out of the cloud to reach for the planes.

Back on the *Kennedy*, Parsons confessed, "I don't think I've ever been so drenched with sweat." He could also report success: The TARPS photographs indicated that Big Al's Place, despite its bristling defenses, would process no uranium for a long, long time.

In fact, almost every possible target in Iraq's entire western des-

As the *John F. Kennedy*'s number-one catapult flung Lieutenant Tom Dostie's A-7 Corsair along the deck toward Iraq on January 24, he felt his plane lurch violently. Something had gone terribly wrong. The pilot of another A-7, sent up to examine the plane, radioed Dostie a sobering report on his landing gear: "The good news is your strut is down and locked; the bad news is there aren't any wheels on the end of it." To get back on deck, Dostie would have to make an emergency barricade landing.

Circling at low altitude, he watched while yellow shirts moved jets to the bow of the aircraft carrier and raised the two jet-blast deflectors to wall off the foredeck from the spot where he was to land. As they had practiced daily *(left)*, about a hundred seamen spread out the rectangular nylon barricade and connected it first to a thick wire rope that crosses the flight deck and works like the carrier's arresting cable and then to a pair of stanchions built into either side of the landing area. Then the stanchions were raised to their twenty-four-foot height, and the men winched the barricade taut.

Dostie executed a six-mile straight-in approach. Upon landing, the A-7 caught one of the arresting cables and plowed into the barricade, which yanked the plane to a stop *(below)*.

Although Lieutenant Dostie, unharmed, would fly again soon, the landing was to be the Corsair's last. A couple of weeks later, after having yielded $3 million in parts, the old war-horse got a twenty-one-gun salute and a gentle push into the Red Sea.

Words of encouragement spelled out in red tape on the belly of an Air Force KC-135 brightened the day of F-14 pilot Lieutenant James Kuhn and his radar intercept officer, Lieutenant Commander David Parsons. "We were just sitting there, lost in our thoughts," Parsons recalled. Then they noticed the message from the tanker crew. "Next thing I know," said Parsons, who took this photograph, "our airplane's shaking, because we're laughing so hard."

ert had been struck, many more than once. "It was very interesting to watch the terrain change below you," said an F-14 RIO from the *America*. "As the war went on, the bridges all went away, got wiped out." Thus, three aircraft carriers were no longer needed in the Red Sea, and on February 8, the *America* began speeding south around the Arabian Peninsula into the Persian Gulf. On Valentine's Day, she joined the *Ranger*, the *Midway*, and the *Theodore Roosevelt* in obliterating Saddam Hussein's navy and degrading his occupation forces in Kuwait.

The Zulu Warriors

The four A-6 Intruders from the USS *Ranger* were only 500 feet off the water and blazing in at 450 knots. On they came, sweeping over Bubiyan Island at the mouth of the Shatt al Arab, the waterway marking the border between Iraq and Iran. It was 5:00 a.m. on January 17, the first blush of dawn showing in the east. Along with thirty other strikers from the *Ranger* and the *Midway*, the Intruders had the honor of raising the curtain on the U.S. Navy's combat operations in the Persian Gulf.

Planners in Riyadh had a keen sense of priority in the selection of targets for these first strikes. As flank guard for the entire Desert Storm campaign, the carrier battle force in the gulf could brook no interference with the gathering American amphibious forces in waters off Kuwait, or with the massive seaborne buildup of ground troops and matériel along the Arabian coast—and certainly not with their own aerial operations. Yet the Iraqis were known to possess numbers of Chinese-supplied Silkworm antiship missiles; their air force included French F-1 Mirage fighter-bombers and Super Frelon helicopters, both of which could serve as launch platforms for the Exocet missiles of Falklands fame; and the Iraqi Navy had numerous missile-armed gunboats and minelaying patrol craft.

To counter these threats, the air tasking order levied F-14 Tomcats from the carriers *Ranger*, *Midway*, and *Theodore Roosevelt* to fly BARCAP (barrier combat air patrol) at two or three of fifteen or more stations up and down the gulf. Aided by U.S. radar planes scrutinizing every takeoff from Iraqi airfields, the Tomcats were to guard against aerial attack. Attack planes from these ships drew assignments to knock out enemy air bases, Silkworm launch sites,

and naval facilities. Of particular concern was the major naval base that lay west of the Shatt al Arab as it emptied through its mile-wide mouth into the Persian Gulf. Umm Qasr by name, the base had been designated as the primary target for the four *Ranger* A-6s.

As the Intruders streaked over Bubiyan Island, thirty miles short of their objective, the first enemy AAA began rising to meet them. "You could see the streaming tracers," said Lieutenant Commander Richard Martin, pilot of the number-four Intruder, "like three or four people on the ground shooting up fire hoses, just in streams. It wasn't too hard to avoid." Accompanying Prowlers, with their potent jammers, had blanked out most of the Iraqi radar, and the SAMs sailed aimlessly—and harmlessly—into the sky. But the antiaircraft artillery—ranging from 30 to 100 millimeters—grew in intensity until it resembled "a solid wall of triple-A," said Martin. "It just didn't look like I could get through there." Flying closer, however, he realized that "the wall had depth to it. You could pick your way around, through the tracers." Martin knew he was safe from tracer rounds that he could see moving, but if one of the blobs of light appeared to be stationary, then he knew that it was "rendezvousing on me," and he rolled his Intruder into a 2.5-G evasive turn.

Ahead of Martin, in the number-three striker, Lieutenant Peter Hunt wove his own way through the curtains of flak. At eight miles from the target, Hunt asked his bombardier-navigator, sitting to his right: "See anything yet?" Gazing intently at his radar screen, Lieutenant Commander Rivers Cleveland could indeed make out through a fog bank the dim outlines of Umm Qasr's square boat basin and its piers. As they pressed in closer, Cleveland could discern the target on his FLIR.

"Let's get the chaff program running," said Hunt. As Cleveland hit the switch that released clouds of aluminum confetti to confuse any enemy radars that might still be operating, Hunt began counting: "Four miles . . . three miles . . . two miles . . . I'm committing." Seconds later, after dropping twelve Rockeye bombs, each filled with 247 bomblets that scattered in all directions, Hunt pulled out of his bombing run and jinked away, racing south. Less than a

INFRARED LINE
SCANNER

PANORAMIC
CAMERA

FRAME
CAMERA

The TARPS pod can hold
three sensors, often a conventional, so-called frame
camera and a panoramic
camera sensitive to ordi-
nary light, plus a scanner
for infrared imaging. Other gear in the pod includes
a defogger for the camer-
as' glass ports, and devices
that move lenses slightly
during exposure to reduce
blurring by adjusting for
the plane's speed.

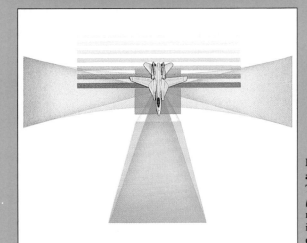

Each TARPS camera has
a unique field of view.
The infrared line scanner
(red) studies terrain di-
rectly below the aircraft
in slivers that extend 60
degrees to both sides of
the plane. Blue shows the
coverage of the panoram-
ic camera—a strip 28 de-
grees wide that extends
from horizon to horizon.
The frame camera (green)
can be aimed to take pic-
tures either straight down
or forward.

For many years, the Navy sent single-purpose jets to get pictures of targets before an air strike and of bomb damage afterward.

The undeniable need for such aircraft, which could neither defend the ship nor attack the enemy, reduced the number of warplanes that a flattop could carry. By the time of Operation Desert Storm, however, a solution had been devised that permitted an F-14 Tomcat to serve as a reconnaissance platform in the morning, then join the fight in the afternoon.

For the recon role, mechanics attach an aerodynamic, seventeen-foot-long aluminum container to the belly of the plane, as shown at left. Called the tactical air reconnaissance pod system, or TARPS, the container holds three cameras, two for visible light and one for infrared. The system enables an F-14 to fly reconnaissance missions at either high or low altitude, by day or night, without compromising the plane's ability to reach supersonic speeds—or to defend itself: Each Peeping Tom, as the TARPS-equipped fighter is called, carries two Sidewinder and two Sparrow air-to-air missiles.

When an aircraft carrier arrives in a trouble spot, three Tomcats are usually assigned to Peeping Tom duty. Depending on the situation, they not only fly prestrike reconnaissance but take on mapping missions, search the area for hostile ships, and perform a spectrum of other tasks as well.

Because the pod is completely integrated with the fighter's computerized weapons system, most TARPS flights resemble strike missions. The pilot, in the front seat, navigates a precise, preplanned track to the target, which appears in standard symbology on his head-up display. Along the way, the radar intercept officer monitors range and time to target and vital camera-control data on a circular tactical information display in the rear cockpit and operates the pod by means of a control panel on his left. And just as during a strike mission, both men must keep a wary eye peeled for enemy surface-to-air missiles and antiaircraft fire.

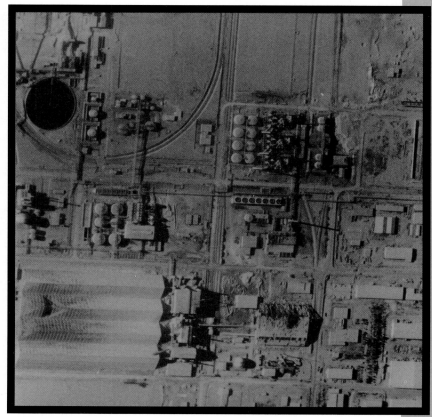

During Operation Desert Storm, an F-14 Peeping Tom took this picture of the Iraqi nuclear facility at Al Qaim with the TARPS panoramic camera. Among other signs of destruction, the photograph shows a building *(bottom center)* **with two large holes punched through the roof.**

minute later, Richard Martin dropped his own Rockeyes and, as he began jinking toward the ship, looked back over his right shoulder to see the bomblets spray into the open hatchway of a small freighter and into a nearby warehouse complex.

All told, twelve Intruders hit Umm Qasr that morning, while other A-6s and F/A-18 Hornets pounded Iraqi port facilities; a pair of enemy airfields; two Silkworm and coastal defense sites; along with a number of radio stations, rail yards, and oil terminals. Despite the ferocity of the AAA, every plane returned safely to the *Ranger* and the *Midway*. However, the enemy installations—and Umm Qasr in particular—would require multiple visits, and on the next night's mission against the naval base, a *Ranger* A-6E was shot down by AAA fire while laying mines across the harbor in front of the naval base. Both crewmen were later declared killed in action.

After day two of the air war, the gulf strikers, like those operating from the Red Sea, discarded low-level tactics. With the assurance that both the high-reaching SAMs and the Iraqi Air Force could be largely neutralized, the attack sorties approached the targets at medium altitude of around 20,000 feet, above the worst of the AAA. Only one more Navy aircraft, a *Roosevelt* A-6 with two crewmen, would be lost in combat.

Again and again, the carrier warplanes struck at Umm Qasr and the other Iraqi naval and missile facilities along the coast. Low clouds and heavy thunderstorms that hindered raids originating in the Red Sea after the first few days of battle hampered the gulf side of the Navy's air war as well. With bomb damage difficult to assess, the Navy simply kept sending in the strikes, the Intruders and Hornets bombing by radar and infrared imaging systems to eradicate missile boats and the Silkworms. On one notable night, an A-6 from the *Roosevelt* drew a bead on a T-shaped pier with six to eight boats tied up to it. Clouds flickered with AAA, but the Intruder dropped its Rockeyes dead on, covering every boat but one at the pier. And as the A-6 jinked away, the crew taped pictures of their infrared screen showing flames shooting from the enemy vessels.

Any Iraqi boat that ventured to sea was likely to come under attack by A-6s, S-3s, and F/A-18s that patrolled some sectors of the gulf virtually around the clock. On January 23, while flying one of these armed surface reconnaissance missions beneath a 4,000-foot overcast, a *Ranger* A-6 spotted an Iraqi craft at the northern edge of the gulf and prepared to attack. In a frantic effort to save itself, the boat raced under a large oil platform. But there was no sanctuary. Diving to 500 feet, the Intruder crew fired a Skipper missile. A hybrid weapon like the SLAM, it consisted of a laser-guided bomb fitted with a rocket motor. The Intruder bombardier-navigator deftly steered it under the platform, where it smashed into the boat. As the Intruder pilot wryly reported, "Hiding under oil platforms is not a tactic that works well against Skipper."

And then, on January 29, Iraq's navy began coming out—out of Umm Qasr, out of Kuwaiti ports, out of the many little inlets that pit the coastline. Commanders Richard Noble and Richard Cassara, pilot and bombardier-navigator of an A-6 from the *Ranger*, entered the naval pantheon as perpetrators of perhaps the slickest trick of the war. They had just completed a successful strike against a Silkworm site in northern Kuwait and still had two of their four 500-pound laser-guided bombs (LGBs) remaining. Hunting around for targets of opportunity near Bubiyan Island, Cassara spotted a large image on his radar that broke into a line of blips as he and Noble drew near. "Hey," called Cassara, "I think we've got a column of four ships. They're heading east at about fifteen to eighteen knots."

Although the shapes were still blurred on the FLIR screen, Cassara thought he could identify three of the vessels as captured Kuwaiti fast missile boats—one FPB 57 and two TNC 45s, each capable of carrying four Exocets. Cassara guessed that the boats were following the lead of the Iraqi Air Force and fleeing to refuge in Iran. "They're only thirteen miles from Iranian waters," Cassara told Noble. "If we don't hit them now they'll get away. The front guy is an FPB 57 for sure. Let's get 'em." So began the end of Iraq's navy.

With only two LGBs remaining, however, Noble and Cassara needed help. Another *Ranger* A-6E on the Silkworm mission responded that it also had a couple of LGBs left, but its FLIR imaging system had failed; with it had gone any opportunity to train the plane's bomb-guiding laser beam on the target. Noble radioed for the A-6E to stand by—in a technique called buddy bombing, the bombs of one plane could home on the laser of another—and dived for the lead Iraqi boat. Cassara positioned his laser-designating reticle on the FLIR image of the vessel just aft of its stack, where the Exocets were mounted. Down screamed the Intruder. As the bombing computer released the weapon, Noble cried "Bomb!" Then he hauled the Intruder into a climbing turn. Simultaneously, Cassara guided the bomb with a control called a slew stick to keep the cross hairs on the target as the A-6 maneuvered. A point of infrared light, created by heat from a chemical generator aboard the bomb used to power its steering vanes, stabbed down the face of his FLIR screen toward the boat. Outside, the A-6 crews could see a huge eruption of orange flame as the LGB exploded amid the Exocets.

In an effort to escape, one of the three other vessels turned to starboard, the second to port, and the third reversed course and made for Iraq at top speed. Noble and Cassara made a run at this boat, hit it amidships, and blew it out of the water.

Now Noble summoned the other Intruder. "Okay," he radioed the crew, "we'll set up for a shallow diving attack on these guys. When I call 'Pickle,' punch off your bomb and we'll guide it in." As the two planes howled down in formation, Cassara fixed one of the boats with his laser designator and waited for the computer to command release. At precisely the right moment, Noble called "Pickle!" and the other A-6 unleashed an LGB. The bomb struck the stern of the vessel and ignited its missiles in a volcanic fireball.

As the Intruders set up to demolish the fourth boat, Cassara's FLIR also began acting up, and the Intruders decided to call off the attack. However, the boat would not get away, for at that moment, two Canadian CF-18 Hornets appeared on the scene and riddled it with bursts of 20-mm cannon fire, sinking the craft in short order.

Ignoring the dismal fate of the little flotilla, other Iraqi boats continued to stream toward Iran, and other carrier and coalition planes joined in the turkey shoot. Within forty-eight hours, nearly forty Iraqi vessels had been sunk or so severely damaged as to be unserviceable, and in days to come, the remains of Saddam Hussein's hapless navy would be annihilated as well. At one time or another, just about every type of aircraft came up to bat. In mid-February, an F/A-18 Hornet flying armed sur-

Thick smoke billows from the bow of an Iraqi oil tanker sunk by A-6 Intruders off the coast of Kuwait on January 2

face reconnaissance nailed a boat with three 1,000-pound bombs, then dived down and strafed the burning hulk for good measure. A few days later, on February 20, a twin-engine Viking, perhaps the world's best submarine hunter but definitely no dive bomber, came across a fleeing Iraqi gunboat, nosed over, and dropped three 500-pound Mark 82 bombs from 17,000 feet. Scratch one boat. And on more than one occasion, F-14 fighter jockeys found a way to relieve their frustration at finding no MiGs to fight. Directed toward Iraqi vessels by airborne controllers, they ripped down to chew up the boats with their 6,000-round-per-minute 20-mm cannons.

The Iraqis were using the ship to provide early warning of air raids launched from carriers in the Persian Gulf.

In the early weeks of the war, the carrier battle force operated prudently in the southern gulf near Bahrain and Qatar, between 360 miles and 400 miles from the nearest Iraqi threat. Such distances required the same sort of lengthy planning and perfect coordination with aerial tankers as did the Red Sea missions. As Saddam's navy was destroyed, however, and his air force intimidated, the battle groups moved north in three jumps of 60 to 100 miles each until they were within easy range of their targets. Relatively short-range F/A-18 Hornets still profited from refueling, but the aging A-6 Intruder could make it to the target and back on one tank of fuel.

Now, the nature of the operations changed, and the pace picked up dramatically. Although the carrier air groups continued to fly BARCAP and armed recon missions over the gulf and to pound Umm Qasr and other installations ashore, the weight of the attack increasingly fell on the enemy army in Kuwait and southern Iraq. After the *America* arrived from the Red Sea on February 14, the hammer blows took on the quality of a kettledrum crescendo.

Some carriers were cycling as many as a dozen strike packages a day aimed at concentrations of tanks, trucks, troops, and artillery. These battlefield suppression strikes obviously did not require the same level of planning as the

Four F/A-18 Hornets, the tips of their folded wings fitted with Sidewinder missiles, share cramped quarters on the flight deck of the carrier *America*. A CH-46 Sea Knight replenishment helicopter approaches through the haze.

long, complex Red Sea missions, where "you'd be in strike planning for hours and hours and hours," a flier from the *America* explained. "You'd have pictures of the target, laying out all these routes, organizing all these aircraft." In the gulf, however, "You'd walk in and they'd say, 'These are the coordinates. You'll end up with something in this area.' And that was the extent of what you got in intelligence." Said one of his shipmates: "You take four A-6s and go. We'd just press right into the country, drop our bombs, come right back, and by the time we've got the engines shut down on the ship they're loading more bombs back on. The pilot's sitting there waiting to climb back inside."

New traditions arise quickly in wartime. On the *Ranger*, the *William Tell* Overture—theme of the old "Lone Ranger" television program—resounded over the loudspeakers each time the ship launched a strike, day or night. Reporters on board asked the crew if they ever got tired of it. The answer was no. "It was neat," said one enthused aviator. "I'd be lying in bed, and it would go off. And it was just a neat sensation."

With missions launching every couple of hours, mess halls were open around the clock, and as on the Red Sea carriers, almost any able-bodied seaman might turn into a temporary ordie. Maintenance, as measured by aircraft-readiness rates, could hardly have been better. Young men not long out of high school—the average age of a carrier crew, including the skipper, is under twenty-one—kept more than 90 percent of their airplanes ready to go when scheduled. Few jets, once airborne, returned to the flight deck because of mechanical or electronic failures. Many a squadron racked up a sortie-completion rate of 98 percent.

Even so, a handful of aircraft fell victim to broken equipment. Perhaps the most noteworthy of these operational losses occurred February 15 on the *America*. Returning from a predawn strike at a Silkworm missile site on Failaka Island off the Kuwaiti coast, an Intruder driver landed his plane in good form. After unhooking from the cable, the pilot had just begun to taxi when the aircraft inexplicably lost its hydraulics. No brakes.

Realizing that their A-6 was headed overboard, the pilot and his bombardier-navigator instantly ejected—and a few seconds later hit the deck, chutes billowing in the thirty-knot wind and dragging them helplessly across the flight deck. Only quick thinking by deck hands saved the fliers from being smashed into parked planes or carried overboard. "When the plane came in," one of the rescuers said later, "we heard two pops go off. We looked up, and the pilots had terror on their faces. Their expressions said 'Do something! Help me out!' I pounced onto the parachute." The pilot broke an ankle; his bombardier-navigator escaped with cuts and abrasions, and was flying again within a week.

The ATOs flown daily to the carriers from Central Command head-quarters in Riyadh now divided target areas in southern Iraq and Kuwait into "kill boxes." Within these thirty-mile squares, Navy Intruders and Hornets joined Air Force, Marine, and other coalition attack squadrons in destroying anything that moved or showed up on the sensors. "Just for example," said one A-6 pilot, "we might be assigned to kill box Alpha Golf 7, so we'd navigate our way up there and show up with a full load. You just kind of keep looking around for the right target, and go, 'Aha! There's one!' and let him have, say, half the gravity bombs on one run, half the next run, and then try to find a tank or an armored personnel carrier—something hot in revetment—for a laser-guided bomb."

Orchestrating the show for the Navy—and feeling a little like air-traffic controllers at Los Angeles International Airport during rush hour—were the E-2C Hawkeyes, four or five from each carrier, orbiting slowly over the gulf. Said the executive officer of the *America*'s Hawkeye squadron: "We're talking to the battle group commander, talking to the ships, talking to the flight leads of the strike, talking to the AWACS, talking to other E-2Cs."

At four o'clock on the morning of February 24, Operation Desert Storm entered its climactic stage as coalition ground forces surged forward, smashed through Iraqi defenses, and rushed ahead so rapidly that air controllers could barely keep up with events.

To prevent allied troops from coming under friendly air attack, a line was drawn well ahead of the advance expected during the next several hours. Called the fire support coordination line (FSCL), it marked a zone of ambiguity where either friendly or enemy troops might be found. Coalition planes were forbidden to attack anything south of the FSCL unless instructed to do so by a forward air controller. Before the assault, planners established an entire series of FSCLs to be used sequentially as the action advanced. Yet so rapidly did the ground forces flood into enemy-held territory that an FSCL sometimes became outdated almost as soon as it was activated. On the *Ranger,* aircrews were briefed to strike north of FSCL 1 about four hours after the ground war began. But as they walked to their planes, the air wing operations officer dashed up with new orders canceling FSCL 1 and establishing FSCL 3 as the operative foul line.

During the ground war, such changes occurred frequently. "We'd call the strike group as they were leaving the ship," an E-2C crew member recalled, "and we'd say, 'Okay, we're changing the target. Your target is now a column of tanks rolling down this road, at this particular coordinate, and you're cleared in from Time X to Time Z—you have a fifteen-minute window. Go in there and drop your bombs.''

Go in and drop them they did, and

Watched by silver-suited fire-fighters, a crash crew on the *America* readies a crane for an effort to pull an A-6 Intruder from steel safety netting beneath the forward edge of the landing area. The brakes had failed after the plane unhooked from the arresting gear cable, sending it slithering over the side. The *America's* skipper ordered the Intruder pushed overboard after learning that, with aircraft due to land, the salvage effort would take several hours.

before long, thousands of Iraqi troops began throwing down their weapons and raising their hands as soon as planes appeared in the sky above. "A lot of times," an F/A-18 pilot later recalled, "we'd be ready to drop the bombs and the forward air controller would say, 'Abort! Abort! They've just surrendered.'"

So overwhelming was coalition air power that during the final hours of Operation Desert Storm, planes circled, stacked in layers, awaiting a turn to take a whack at a target. Of one mission, an A-6 pilot remembered, "We went about sixty miles into Iraq, looking for something to bomb. I talked to this one controller and he said, 'Well, I've got A-10s at 4,000 feet, F-18s at 6,000 feet, F-16s here, and you above them.'"

And so, on February 27, 1991, when the war in the Persian Gulf ended precisely 100 hours after the ground offensive had begun, the men who had flown from the six aircraft carriers—the *John F. Kennedy*, the *Saratoga*, and the *America*, and the *Ranger*, the *Midway*, and the *Theodore Roosevelt*—were delighted, but they were not particularly surprised. "There was," as one of the aviators put it, "nothing left to fight"—at least not in Kuwait, whose liberation had been achieved.

On March 11, less than two weeks after Desert Storm had come to its inexorable conclusion, the *Saratoga* and the *Midway* battle groups began their majestic parades from the Red

Sea and the Persian Gulf. Yet hardly had the repositioning of U.S. naval might begun than the longstanding debate resumed over the future of the aircraft carrier. Domestic budget constraints and the collapse of Soviet Communist ambitions are almost certain to result in a lower U.S. military profile, with a considerable reduction in naval forces. Some experts see the Navy dropping from 545 active ships in 1991 to 451 by 1995 and perhaps to as few as 310 by the year 2010. Obviously, there will be fewer carrier battle groups.

How many is uncertain, but probably no more than a dozen. Of the fifteen carriers in active service, eight are more than thirty years old. The *Ranger*, for example, is thirty-four, the *Saratoga* thirty-five, and the *Midway* an ancient forty-six. They can still do a job, as the Gulf War so amply demonstrated, but these and other oil-burning flattops cost more to operate than newer, nuclear-powered ships. Most face retirement by the turn of the century or a little later. Replacements: only three nuclear-powered supercarriers—the *George Washington*, the *John C. Stennis*, and the *United States*. A $3.3 billion price tag on each, however, and the need for a like amount to purchase an eighty-five- to ninety-plane air wing for each makes them the subject of great debate.

Some critics hold that the United States would be better and more economically served by updated versions of the British ski-jump carrier *Invincible* and their doughty Harriers or other short-takeoff aircraft. Strongly rejecting that idea, the U.S. Navy points out that the ship carried no airborne early-warning planes like the Hawkeye and no tankers. In addition, goes the argument, Harriers in the Falklands flew against obsolete aircraft under special circumstances that are unlikely to be widely repeated. Furthermore, the technology that lets the Harrier take off and land on a dime is still in its infancy. Though the Soviets reportedly are testing a supersonic, Harrier-like aircraft called the Yak-141, no evidence suggests that it—or anything on the drawing boards—can challenge the U.S. Navy's present-generation F-14 Tomcat or F/A-18 Hornet, either as a fighter or as an attack aircraft.

Size is another important issue. The *Invincible*, argues the Navy, is so small—capable of holding only eight or nine Harriers—that a large number of such ships would be required to serve in the power-projection role of U.S. aircraft carriers, and still they could not approach the capabilities displayed by the six flattops that participated in the Gulf War. Finally, the vulnerability of small carriers

The caravan painted on this A-7 Corsair grew by one camel after each of the plane's forty-two combat missions over Iraq or Kuwait between January 17 and February 28. Nominally assigned to Lieutenant Dano Wise, who flew twenty-three missions during the Gulf War in this and other aircraft, number 407 was piloted by several aviators to keep them from becoming accustomed to any one jet's idiosyncrasies. Weapon silhouettes itemize ordnance dropped.

is equal to that of large ones, and defending them offers no less challenge.

During the Cold War, the Navy saw a role for its aircraft carriers in attacking the Soviet Union where it was accessible to sea-launched aircraft. In the late 1980s, the Soviets beefed up their modest fleet of four 40,000-ton carriers housing a dozen jets each. They completed one 65,000-ton ship with room for sixty-five aircraft and began work on two more of similar dimensions. Given the recent military retrenchment of the Soviets, however, a World War II-style clash between the rival fleets appears unlikely. The Navy will have to find new justification for the immense expenditures demanded by these remarkable vessels and their supporting cast of warships. Perhaps the rationale will lie in the uncertain new order in the world replacing the familiar if fragile equilibrium of the Cold War. With America's vital interests spread around the globe, the potential remains great for crises that could well prompt a U.S. president to ask: "Where are the carriers?" ★

Acknowledgments

The editors wish to thank the following: Guy Aceto, *Air Force Magazine*, Arlington, Va.; Gina Akers, Navy Yard Historical Center, Washington, D.C.; Tom Bacon, Oceana Naval Air Station, Va.; BMCS Barrett, Norfolk, Va.; Robert C. Beers, General Electric, Moorestown, N.J.; Capt. Lyle Bien, Arlington, Va.; John Boatman, Jane's Defense Publishers, Alexandria, Va.; Comdr. Brian Calhoun, Dept. of the Navy, Washington, D.C.; Mike Carlin, Landenberg, Pa.; Lt. Deborah Carson, Washington, D.C.; Comdr. Joe Connelly, McLean, Va.; Dorothy Cross, Pentagon, Washington, D.C.; Capt. J. P. Day, Norfolk, Va.; Lt. Comdr. Dana Dervay, Oceana Naval Air Station, Va.; Lorna Dodt, Pentagon; Lt. Comdr. George Dom, Dept. of the Navy, Washington, D.C.; Russell D. Egnor, Pentagon; Capt. Kent Ewing, Norfolk, Va.; Lt. (jg) Tony Fox, Oceana Naval Air Station, Va.; Squadron Leader Jeff Glover, RAF Wittering, Cambridgeshire, England; Vadim Gratzianski, Moscow, USSR; Brian Haigh, Huish Episcopi, Somerset, England; Hugh Howard, Pentagon; Lt. Comdr. Gordon Hume, Norfolk, Va.; Lt. Thomas Kane, Oceana Naval Air Station, Va.; Lt. (jg) Taylor Kiland, Pentagon; Lt. Dane LaJoye, Pentagon; Comdr. John Leenhouts, Orange Park, Fla.; Capt. James McFillin, Washington, D.C.; Mike McKenna, Oceana Naval Air Station, Va.; Comdr. Donald McSwain, Dept. of the Navy, Washington, D.C.; Lt. Chuck McWharter, Norfolk, Va.; Lt. Comdr. Richard W. Martin, Oak Harbor, Wash.; Comdr. Mike Maurer, Oceana Naval Air Station, Va.; Capt. Stephen Millikin, The Tailhook Association, Bonita, Calif.; Irene Miner, Pentagon; Lyle Minter, Pentagon; Capt. Jim Mitchell, Washington, D.C.; Group Captain Sid Morris, RAF Wittering, Cambridgeshire, England; Ronald O'Rourke, Congressional Research Service, Washington, D.C.; Dave Parkyn, Plymouth, Devon, England; Chuck Porter, Dept. of Defense, Washington, D.C.; Capt. Steven Ramsdell, Silverdale, Wash.; Capt. Rosario M. Rausa, Association of Naval Aviation, Falls Church, Va.; Comdr. Anthony Reade, Oceana Naval Air Base, Va.; Capt. Carter Refo, Carrier Readiness Program, Washington, D.C.; John Reilly, Jr., U.S. Navy Historical Center, Washington, D.C.; Lt. David Roller, Oceana Naval Air Station, Va.; William Rosenmund, Pentagon; Lt. Robert Ross, Washington, D.C.; Reenie Shea, San Diego *Union*, San Diego, Calif.; Lt. Chuck Shirley, Norfolk, Va.; Lt. Comdr. Craig Smith, Norfolk, Va.; Eric Solander, General Dynamics, Rancho Cucamonga, Calif.; Bud Spencer, Oceana Naval Air Station, Va.; Comdr. Edward Stafford (Ret.), Chester, Md.; Harold Stubbs, Norfolk, Va.; Mabel Thomas, Pentagon; Scott C. Truver, Techmatics, Inc., Arlington, Va.; Comdr. Bill Tyson, Norfolk, Va.; Comdr. T. Ladson Webb, Norfolk, Va.; Comdr. T. Ladson Webb, Norfolk, Va.; Mike White, Oceana Naval Air Station, Va.; Mack Williams and Lt. Mike Winslow, Oceana Naval Air Station, Va.; A.O.2 Paul Woods, Norfolk, Va.; Lt. David Wray, Naval Base, Guam.

Bibliography

BOOKS

Allen, Thomas B., F. Clifton Berry, and Norman Polmar, *CNN: War in the Gulf.* Atlanta, Ga.: Turner Publishing, 1991.

Bishop, Chris, ed., *The Encyclopedia of World Sea Power.* New York: Crescent Books, 1988.

Bonds, Ray, ed., *Modern Carriers.* New York: Prentice Hall Press, 1988.

Brown, David, *The Royal Navy and the Falklands War.* London: Leo Cooper, 1987.

Burden, Rodney, et al., *Falklands: The Air War.* London: Arms and Armour Press, 1986.

Carver, Michael, *War Since 1945.* Atlantic Highlands, N.J.: Ashfield Press, 1990.

Chant, Christopher, *Air Defense Systems and Weapons.* Washington, D.C.: Brassey's Defense Publishers, 1989.

Corse, Carl D., Jr., *Introduction to Shipboard Weapons.* Annapolis, Md.: Naval Institute Press, 1975.

Dartford, Mark, ed., *Falklands Armoury.* Poole, Dorset, England: Blandford Press, 1985.

Dorr, Robert F., *Vietnam MiG Killers.* Osceola, Wis.: Motorbooks International, 1988.

Elsam, Group Capt. M. B., *Air Defence.* London: Brassey's, 1989.

Ethell, Jeffrey, and Alfred Price, *Air War South Atlantic.* New York: Macmillan, 1983.

Fitzsimons, Bernard, *Aces High.* London: Salamander Books, 1988.

Francillon, René J., *Vietnam: The War in the Air.* New York: Arch Cape Press, 1987.

Friedman, Norman,
Carrier Air Power. Annapolis, Md.: Naval Institute Press, 1981.
Desert Victory: The War for Kuwait. Annapolis, Md.: Naval Institute Press, 1991.
The Naval Institute Guide to World Naval Weapons Systems. Annapolis, Md.: Naval Institute Press, 1989.
The Postwar Naval Revolution. Annapolis, Md.: Naval Institute Press, 1986.
"Providing Defense against Anti-Ship Missiles." In *The International Countermeasures Handbook.* Englewood, Colo.: Cardiff Publishing, 1990.
U.S. Aircraft Carriers. Annapolis, Md.: Naval Institute Press, 1983.
The U.S. Maritime Strategy. London, England: Jane's Publishing, 1988.
U.S. Naval Weapons. Annapolis, Md.: Naval Institute Press, 1988.

Friedrich, Otto, ed., and the Editors of Time, *Desert Storm: The War in the Persian Gulf.* New York: Time Warner Publishing, 1991.

Garrison, Peter, *CV: Carrier Aviation.* Novato, Calif.: Presidio Press, 1980.

Gerken, Louis, *ASW Versus Submarine Technology Battle.* Chula Vista, Calif.: American Scientific Corp., 1986.

Gillcrist, Paul T., *Feet Wet: Reflections of a Carrier Pilot.* New York: Simon & Schuster, 1990.

Godden, John, ed., *Harrier: Ski-Jump to Victory.* Washington, D.C.: Pergamon-Brassey's International Defense Publishers, 1983.

Grove, Eric, ed., *NATO's Defence of the North.* Washington, D.C.: Pergamon-Brassey's International Defense Publishers, 1989.

Gunston, Bill, *Modern Fighting Aircraft: Harrier.* New York: Arco Publishing, 1984.

Hastings, Max, and Simon Jenkins, *The Battle for the Falklands.* New York: W. W. Norton, 1983.

Heatley, C. J., III, *The Cutting Edge.* Charlottesville,

Va.: Thomasson-Grant, 1986.

Hill, Rear Adm. J. R.:
 Air Defence at Sea. Surrey, England: Ian Allen Ltd., 1988.
 Anti-Submarine Warfare. Annapolis, Md.: Naval Institute Press, 1985. ·

Hoyt, Edwin P., *Carrier Wars.* New York: McGraw-Hill, 1989.

Hughes, Capt. Wayne P., Jr., *Fleet Tactics: Theory and Practice.* Annapolis, Md.: Naval Institute Press, 1986.

An Illustrated Guide to the Techniques and Equipment of Electronic Warfare. New York: Arco Publishing, 1985.

Jane's Fighting Ships. Ed. by Capt. Richard Sharpe. Alexandria, Va.: Jane's Information Group, 1990.

Jordan, John, *An Illustrated Guide to the Modern U.S. Navy.* New York: Prentice Hall Press, 1986.

Keegan, John, *The Price of Admiralty: The Evolution of Naval Warfare.* London: Penguin Books, 1988.

Knott, Capt. Richard C., ed., *The Naval Aviation Guide.* Annapolis, Md.: Naval Institute Press, 1988. ·

Maroon, Fred J., and Edward L. Beach, *Keepers of the Sea.* Annapolis, Md.: Naval Institute Press, 1983.

Middlebrook, Martin:
 The Fight for the 'Malvinas.' London: Penguin Group, 1989.
 Task Force: The Falklands War, 1982. London: Penguin Group, 1987.

The Military Frontier, by the Editors of Time-Life Books (Understanding Computers series). Alexandria, Va.: Time-Life Books, 1988.

Miller, David, and John Jordan, *Modern Submarine Warfare.* London: Salamander Books, 1987.

Miller, David, and Chris Miller, *Modern Naval Combat.* New York: Crescent Books, 1986.

Modern Fighting Aircraft: F-14 Tomcat. New York: Prentice Hall Press, 1985.

Nichols, Comdr. John B., and Barrett Tillman, *On Yankee Station.* Annapolis, Md.: Naval Institute Press, 1987.

Nitze, Paul H., Leonard Sullivan, Jr., et al., *Securing the Seas: The Soviet Naval Challenge and Western Alliance Options.* Boulder, Colo.: Westview Press, 1979.

Peacock, Lindsay, *F-14 Tomcat Squadrons of the U.S. Navy.* London: Ian Allan, 1986.

Perkins, Maj. Gen. K., ed., *Weapons and Warfare.* London: Brassey's, 1987.

Polmar, Norman, *CNN: War in the Gulf.* Atlanta, Ga.: Turner Publishing, 1991.

Prézelin, Bernard, ed., *The Naval Institute Guide to Combat Fleets of the World, 1990-91.* Annapolis, Md.: Naval Institute Press, 1990.

Reynolds, Clark G., and the Editors of Time-Life Books, *The Carrier War* (The Epic of Flight series). Alexandria, Va.: Time-Life Books, 1982.

Shaw, Robert L., *Fighter Combat: Tactics and Maneuvering.* Annapolis, Md.: Naval Institute Press, 1985.

Sundt, Capt. Wilbur A., *Naval Science.* Annapolis, Md.: Naval Institute Press, 1980.

Sweetman, Bill, *U.S. Naval Airpower.* Osceola, Wis.: Motorbooks International, 1987.

Terzibaschitsch, Stefan, *Aircraft Carriers of the U.S. Navy.* Annapolis, Md.: Naval Institute Press, 1989.

Till, Geoffrey, *Modern Sea Power: An Introduction.* London: Brassey's Defense Publishers, 1987.

Van Deurs, Rear Adm. George, *Wings for the Fleet.* Annapolis, Md.: Naval Institute Press, 1966.

Watson, Bruce W., *Red Navy at Sea: Soviet Naval Operations on the High Seas, 1956-1980.* Boulder, Colo.: Westview Press, 1982.

Watson, Bruce W., and Susan M. Watson, *The Soviet Navy: Strengths and Liabilities.* Boulder, Colo.: Westview Press, 1986.

Woodward, Bob, *The Commanders.* New York: Simon & Schuster, 1991.

PERIODICALS

Andrews, Hal, "Ready or Not: Naval Aviation's Aircraft and Ships on the Eve of Pearl Harbor." *Naval Aviation News,* January-February 1990.

Andrews, Peter, and the Editors of American Heritage:
 "Embattled Heritage: 1946 to the Present." *Navy Air,* 1986.
 "Sailors in the Sky: The Beginning to 1918." *Navy Air,* 1986.

Boatman, John, "U.S. Navy Facing Air Defence Gap." *Jane's Defence Weekly,* March 2, 1991.

Burgess, Lt. Comdr. Rick, "The Tomcat at 20." *Naval Aviation News,* January-February 1991.

Burgess, Tom, "Navy Widens Alert Area to Protect Ships." *Air Force Times,* February 6, 1984.

Carter, Edward W., III:
 "Chess Game." *All Hands* (U.S. Navy), October 1989.
 "Combat Vulnerability: So What's New?" *Proceedings* (U.S. Naval Institute), May 1988.
 "Countering Anti-Ship Missiles." *Defense Electronics,* September 1990.

Doerner, William R., "Tangling with Tehran." *Time,* May 2, 1988.

Dorsey, Jack, "New Technology Lets Navy Pilots SLAM It to Iraq at Safer Distance." *Virginian-Pilot,* January 22, 1991.

Dunleavy, Vice Adm. Dick, "Ready When Called." *Naval Aviation News,* November-December 1990.

Eckholm, Erik, "In Détente and Cutbacks, Navy Has Potential Foes." *New York Times,* May 22, 1990.

Evans, Julius L., "Eject!" *Air Combat,* April 1991.

Ewing, Steve, "Development of the U.S. Navy's Aircraft Carriers to 1961." *Foundation* (Pensacola, Fla.), spring 1990.

Friedman, Norman, "The *Vincennes* Incident." *Proceedings* (U.S. Naval Institute), May 1989.

Goodman, Glenn W., Jr., "*Vincennes* Tragedy Could Be Repeated Closer to Home." *Armed Forces Journal International,* July 1989.

Graves, William S., "The Human Side of the *Forrestal* Disaster." *Navy: The Magazine of Sea Power,* November 1967.

Greeley, Brendan M., Jr., "U.S. Sinks Iranian Frigate in Persian Gulf Action." *Aviation Week & Space Technology,* April 25, 1988.

Gross, Richard C., "Lessons Learned the Hard Way: The USS *Stark.*" *Defense Science and Electronics,* December 1987.

Hewish, Mark, Bill Sweetman, and Anthony Robinson, "Precision-Guided Munitions Come of Age." *International Defense Review,* May 1991.

Hornik, Richard, "When Attackers Become Targets." *Time,* June 1, 1987.

Houseman, Damian, "Anti-Submarine Warfare: The Deadly Game," *International Defense Images,* 1986.

Kelly, Lt. Comdr. Scott, "Carrier ASW: Can Do." *Proceedings* (U.S. Naval Institute), January 1990.

Kitfield, James, "How Survivable Are Today's Ships?" *Military Logistics Forum,* March 1987.

Lake, Rear Adm. Julian S., "Shooting vs. Jamming." *Armed Forces Journal International,* April 1991.

Lamar, Jacob V., Jr., "Why Did This Happen?" *Time*, June 1, 1987.

Langston, Capt. Bud, and Lt. Comdr. Don Bringle, "The Air View: Operation Praying Mantis," *Proceedings* (U.S. Naval Institute), May 1989.

Lightbody, Andy, "The Carrier Battle Group," *International Defense Images*, 1986.

MacFarquhar, Neil, "Carrier's Crew Responds to Gulf War's Call." *Stars & Stripes*, January 21, 1991.

McKearney, Lt. Comdr. T. K., "Safeguarding the Sitting Ducks." *Proceedings* (U.S. Naval Institute), December 1984.

Magnuson, Ed, "A Shouted Alarm, A Fiery Blast." *Time*, June 1, 1987.

Meyer, Mark, "Going Up to Big Al." *Proceedings* (U.S. Naval Institute), July 1991.

Morello, Carol, "On a Carrier, Bravado—and Grace under Pressure." *Philadelphia Inquirer*, January 27, 1991.

Morrocco, John D., "Naval Aviation Plan Sacrifices Some Capability To Avoid Further Cuts in Aircraft Carriers." *Aviation Week & Space Technology*, May 6, 1991.

O'Keefe, Lt. Comdr. James G., and Lt. Comdr. David L. Hallenbeck, "Protecting the Carrier against Torpedo Attack." *Naval War College Review*, January-February 1982.

Perkins, Capt. J. B., III, "Operation Praying Mantis." *Proceedings* (U.S. Naval Institute), May 1989.

"The Persian Gulf Ablaze." *Defence Update*, July 1988.

Reid, W. W., "Flight of the Editor." *All Hands* (Alexandria, Va.), December 1989.

Rizzuto, Timothy C., "Vulcan/Phalanx: An Effective Close-in Weapon System?" *Proceedings* (U.S. Naval Institute), September 1976.

Rodrigue, George, "Never Mind Those Fighter Planes." *Virginian-Pilot*, February 18, 1991.

"SLAMs Hit Iraqi Target in First Combat Firing." *Aviation Week & Space Technology*, January 28, 1991.

Steigman, David S., "Meyer Brought Aegis to Life in Cornfield." *Navy Times*, May 20, 1981.

Vlahos, Michael, "The *Stark* Report." *Proceedings* (U.S. Naval Institute), May 1988.

Wheeler, Gerald E., "Naval Aviation's First Year." *Proceedings* (U.S. Naval Institute), May 1961.

"Who Are All Those People on the Platform?" *Inside Approach* (Norfolk, Va.), October 1988.

Wilhelm, Lt. Ross M., "Live by the Sword, Die by the Swordsmen." *The Hook*, summer 1991.

Zumwalt, Adm. Elmo R., Jr., "Naval Battles We Could Lose." *International Security Review*, summer 1981.

OTHER SOURCES

"America's Carrier Battle Groups: Lasting Requirements in a Period of Global Change." Booklet. Falls Church, Va.: Information Spectrum, Inc., March 1, 1991.

"Anti-Submarine Warfare: Meeting the Challenge." Booklet. Washington, D.C.: Chief of Naval Operations, 1990.

"Flight Deck Awareness." Booklet. Norfolk, Va.: Naval Safety Center, no date.

Fox, Lt. Comdr. Mark I., and Lt. Nicholas Mongillo, interviews. U.S. Navy, no date.

"Marine Fire Prevention, Firefighting and Fire Safety." Booklet. Washington, D.C.: U.S. Department of Commerce, Maritime Administration, 1980.

"Navy Fact File." Booklet. Washington, D.C.: U.S. Dept. of the Navy, no date.

"Navy News, Fire Release" #3, #4, and others. Press Releases. New York: USS *Forrestal* Public Affairs Office, Dept. of the Navy, 1967.

O'Rourke, Ronald, "The Cost of a U.S. Navy Aircraft Carrier Battle Group." Booklet. Washington, D.C.: U.S. Library of Congress, June 26, 1987.

Pool Report. Washington, D.C.: Dept. of the Navy, January 1991.

Russell, James S., "Final Report of Panel to Report Safety in Carrier Operations," Post-46 Command File, Individual Personnel, Operational Archives, Naval Historical Center. Washington, D.C.: Dept. of the Navy, October 16, 1967.

"The Shield and the Storm." Supplement to *Wings of Gold*. Falls Church, Va.: The Association of Naval Aviation, June 10, 1991.

"Still Making History: Naval Aviation." Fact Sheet. Norfolk, Va.: Public Affairs Office of USS *Theodore Roosevelt*, no date.

"Storm Watch." Booklet. Washington, D.C.: Dept. of the Navy, 1991.

U.S. Congress, Congressional Budget Office. *Future Budget Requirements for the 600-Ship Navy*. Washington, D.C.: U.S. Government Printing Office, September 1985.

U.S. Congress, House of Representatives, Committee on Armed Services. *Report on the Staff Investigation into the Iraqi Attack on the USS Stark*. Washington, D.C.: U.S. Government Printing Office, 1987.

U.S. Congress, House of Representatives, Committee on Armed Services, *Ship Survivability*. Washington, D.C.: U.S. Government Printing Office, 1988.

"The United States Navy in 'Desert Shield,' 'Desert Storm.'" Booklet. Washington, D.C.: Dept. of the Navy, May 15, 1991.

"The World's Missile Systems." Booklet. Pomona, Calif.: General Dynamics, August 1988.

Index

Picture Credits

The sources for the illustrations that appear in this book are listed below. Credits from left to right are separated by semicolons; from top to bottom they are separated by dashes.

Cover: Grumman Corporation. 6, 7: Alain Ernoult, Paris. 8, 9: © Robert L. Lawson/Tailhook Photo Service. 10, 11: Lt. Comdr. Kenneth P. Neubauer. 12, 13: U.S. Navy/Lt. Comdr. Dave Parsons, DN-ST-91-02739. 14, 15: Mi Seitelman/Foto Consortium. 16: U.S. Navy/PH3 Frank A. Marquart, DN-SC-91-00650. 20, 21: Mike Nelson/Agence France Presse. 23: U.S. Navy, NH-82737. 24, 25: U.S. Navy, courtesy Tailhook Photo Service. 26, 27: John Batchelor, Wimborne, Dorset, England. 28: U.S. Navy, DN-SC-87-06412. 32, 33: U.S. Navy/PH1 Rodney K. Bean, DN-SC-90-08902. 34, 35: Map by Mapping Specialists; art by Alfred T. Kamajian. 36, 37: Art by Alfred T. Kamajian (2). 40, 41: U.S. Navy/Lt. Comdr. Art Legare, DN-SC-89-07551. 42, 43: U.S. Navy, DN-SN-89-03126; DN-SN-89-03122. 47: U.S. Navy/PH3 Chester O. Falkenhainer, SP-90-00342A—San Diego Union/John McCutchen. 48, 49: Lt. Comdr. Dave Parsons. 50: U.S. Navy, DN-SC-86-07436. 54: Giorgio Arra. 56, 57: General Dynamics, Air Defense Systems

Division; Department of Defense, KN-23720. 58, 59: William G. Lotz. 60, 61: Ned Baumer, courtesy The Tailhook Association. 64, 65: William G. Lotz. 66, 67: New Orleans Times-Picayune/Ted Jackson. 68: David Hathcox/Arms Communications (2)—Fred J. Maroon (2); David Hathcox/Arms Communications. 70, 71: San Diego Union/John McCutchen; Lans Stout; San Diego Union/John McCutchen—Harry Gerwein/Foto Consortium. 72, 73: Lans Stout; Gary Kieffer/Foto Consortium; George Hall/Check Six—Lans Stout. 74, 75: David Hathcox/Arms Communications; Neil Leifer; © Robert L. Lawson/Tailhook Photo Service—David Hathcox/Arms Communications. 76, 77: Lt. Comdr. Kenneth P. Neubauer—Robert F. Dorr. 78, 79: David Hathcox/Arms Communications; Kirby Harrison/Foto Consortium. 80, 81: Lans Stout (4)—David Hathcox/Arms Communications. 82: Jeff Ethell/Foto Consortium. 84, 85: Map by Mapping Specialists. 86-91: Press Association, London. 93: Jeff Ethell/Foto Consortium. 94, 95: British Crown Copyright, 1991/MOD—art by Mark Robinson. 98, 99: British Crown Copyright, 1991/MOD; Press Association, London. 101: Sub-Lt. Dibb's Private Collection—AP/Wide World—Imperial War Museum, London. 104, 105: Press Association, London. 107: British Crown Copyright, 1991/MOD. 108, 109: Press Association, London (2). 110, 111: Fleet Air Arm Museum, RNAS Yeovilton, Somerset, England. 112: *Philadelphia Inquirer*/Todd Buchanan. 116, 117: New Orleans *Times-Picayune*/Ted Jackson. 118, 119: William G. Lotz; David Hathcox/Arms Communications; William G. Lotz. 121: Map by Mapping Specialists. 122, 123: *Philadelphia Inquirer*/Todd Buchanan. 124, 125: U.S. Navy/PH3 Eric James, DN-ST-91-05650. 128, 129: U.S. Air Force/MSgt. Timothy Hadryck. 130, 131: U.S. Navy/PHAN E. Ortega, DN-SC-89-09949; art by Alfred T. Kamajian. 132, 133: U.S. Navy/Comdr. John Leenhouts. 136, 137: Dave Parsons/Blue Thunder Pictures—U.S. Navy/ PH2 Charles W. Moore. 138, 139: Lt. Comdr. Dave Parsons. 140, 141: Lt. Comdr. Dave Parsons—art by Mark Robinson (2); U.S. Navy. 144, 145: U.S. Navy/PH2 Robert Clare, DS-571728. 146, 147: New Orleans *Times-Picayune*/Ted Jackson. 150, 151: U.S. Navy/PHAA Posnecker. 153: U.S. Navy/PH3 Paul A. Hawthorne.

Time-Life Books
is a division of Time Life Inc.,
a wholly owned subsidiary of
THE TIME INC. BOOK COMPANY

TIME-LIFE BOOKS

PRESIDENT: Mary N. Davis

MANAGING EDITOR: Thomas H. Flaherty
Director of Editorial Resources: Elise D. Ritter-Clough
Director of Photography and Research:
John Conrad Weiser
Editorial Board: Dale M. Brown, Roberta Conlan, Laura Foreman, Lee Hassig, Jim Hicks, Blaine Marshall, Rita Thievon Mullin, Henry Woodhead
Assistant Director of Editorial Resources/Training Manager: Norma E. Shaw

PUBLISHER: Robert H. Smith

Associate Publisher: Ann M. Mirabito
Editorial Director: Russell B. Adams, Jr.
Marketing Director: Anne C. Everhart
Production Manager: Prudence G. Harris
Supervisor of Quality Control: James King

Editorial Operations
Production: Celia Beattie
Library: Louise D. Forstall
Computer Composition: Deborah G. Tait (Manager), Monika D. Thayer, Janet Barnes Syring, Lillian Daniels
Interactive Media Specialist: Patti H. Cass

Correspondents: Elisabeth Kraemer-Singh (Bonn); Christine Hinze (London); Christina Lieberman (New York); Maria Vincenza Aloisi (Paris); Ann Natanson (Rome). Valuable assistance was also provided by Juan Sosa (Moscow), Elizabeth Brown and Katheryn White (New York).

THE NEW FACE OF WAR

SERIES EDITOR: Lee Hassig
Series Administrator: Judith W. Shanks

Editorial Staff for *Carrier Warfare*
Art Director: Fatima Taylor
Picture Editor: Marion Ferguson Briggs
Text Editor: Stephen G. Hyslop
Writer: Charles J. Hagner
Associate Editor/Research: Robin Currie
Assistant Editors/Research: Dan Kulpinski, Mark Rogers
Assistant Art Director: Sue Ellen Pratt
Senior Copy Coordinator: Elizabeth Graham
Picture Coordinator: David Beard
Editorial Assistant: Kathleen S. Walton

Special Contributors: Champ Clark, George Constable, George Daniels, John Leigh, M. Allen Paul III, Anthony K. Pordes, Craig Roberts, Christine Soares, Diane Ullius (text); Doug Brown, Catherine Halesky, Annette Scarpitta, John Turnbull, Kathy Wismar (research); Mel Ingber (index).

Library of Congress Cataloging in Publication Data
Carrier warfare/by the editors of Time-Life Books.
    p. cm.   (The New face of war).
  Includes bibliographical references and index.
  ISBN 0-8094-8625-3
  1. Aircraft carriers. I. Time-Life Books. II. Series.
V874.C37 1992
359.3'255—dc20   91-9703 CIP
ISBN 0-8094-8626-1 (lib. bdg.)

© 1991 Time-Life Books. All rights reserved. No part of this book may be reproduced in any form or by any electronic or mechanical means, including information storage and retrieval devices or systems, without prior written permission from the publisher, except that brief passages may be quoted for reviews.
First printing. Printed in U.S.A.
Published simultaneously in Canada.
School and library distribution by Silver Burdett Company, Morristown, New Jersey 07960.

TIME-LIFE is a trademark of Time Warner Inc. U.S.A.

WATERLOO HIGH SCHOOL LIBRARY
1464 INDUSTRY RD.
ATWATER, OHIO 44201

Carrier warfare
Time life

12347
359.3 Car